Partner Retirement in Law Firms

Strategies for Partners, Law Firms and Other Professional Services

Editor
Ronnie Fox

Managing director
Sian O'Neill

***Partner Retirement in Law Firms: Strategies for Partners, Law Firms and Other Professional Services* is published by**

Globe Law and Business Ltd
3 Mylor Close
Horsell
Woking
Surrey GU21 4DD
United Kingdom
Tel: +44 20 3745 4770
www.globelawandbusiness.com

Printed and bound in Great Britain by Ashford Colour Press Ltd

Partner Retirement in Law Firms: Strategies for Partners, Law Firms and Other Professional Services

ISBN 9781787423428
EPUB ISBN 9781787423435
Adobe PDF ISBN 9781787423442
Mobi ISBN 9781787423459

Table of contents

Preface

Ronnie Fox
Fox & Partners

Why do partners in professional firms find it so difficult to contemplate, or even talk about, retirement? Having spoken to many partners, I have concluded that the most common reasons are as follows.

First, the practice of most professions is permitted only after the successful completion of lengthy academic, practical and ethical training, during which the subject of eventual retirement is rarely if ever mentioned. Almost everything which I learned at school and at university is completely irrelevant to the practice of law today. Lawyers who qualified more than 30 years ago have had to acquire on-the-job training in many topics relevant to their daily work – artificial intelligence, cybersecurity, financial management, psychology, leadership, delegation, business development, presentation, communication and so on. But not how to retire gracefully; even today, there are relatively few sources of knowledge on the subject of retirement and succession.

Secondly, a thread running through professional life is the importance of placing the interests of clients above one's own personal interests. The pressures of client demands and other aspects of legal work are often so great that practitioners fail to set aside sufficient time to plan their own careers or to adjust for the developments associated with ageing.

Thirdly, addressing the prospect of major life changes makes many people feel uncomfortable. Their identity is intimately related to their work – and to going out to work. They are what they do. Planning for succession and retirement involves facing up to mortality.

This report offers a variety of practical and technical suggestions as to ways in which lawyers and other professionals can plan for an enjoyable retirement. I am extremely grateful to each of the authors (solicitors, accountants, a psychotherapist, a career consultant and a financial adviser) who have generously shared their knowledge by contributing a chapter. The contents of this report reflect the authors' understanding of the law and best practice as at 1 December 2019.

This report is designed to be read from beginning to end; specific cross-references between chapters seem unnecessary. You will not find all the answers in this book, but you may be prompted to ask yourself relevant questions. Seek appropriate expert advice to generate answers applicable to your own personal circumstances. If you do not ask yourself those questions and seek answers, nobody else can be relied on to do so for you.

One unknown faced by those planning to retire is often how their significant other will react. Nearly 30 years ago, in the well-known Blondie comic strip, Kimberly said that her husband had retired a couple of months previously and was now sitting around the house all day driving Kimberley batty. Kimberley insisted, "I married him for better or worse, but not for lunch!".

On a good day, my wife says that she is surprised by how much I am enjoying spending more time at home and with the family – and even more surprised that she is enjoying having me at home...

I. Partner retirement – a firm's perspective

Corinne Staves
Maurice Turnor Gardner LLP

A professional firm can handle a partner's retirement very badly or very smoothly. Most partner exits sit somewhere in between. Firms can usually achieve the latter by sticking to a simple, six-word motto:

Be prepared. Be right. Be nice.

1. Background

This chapter explores some key issues for professional firms when a partner leaves the firm. There are essentially only two routes for a partner to leave a firm:

- voluntary retirement, which includes both end-of-career retirement and moving elsewhere; or
- involuntary expulsion, encompassing expulsion for cause and no-cause removal.

The firm needs to be prepared for both.

2. Be prepared

2.1 Legal framework

(a) Structure

The vast majority of UK professional firms operate as limited liability partnerships (LLPs), although some operate as limited companies and a few remain as general (unlimited liability) partnerships. In the United Kingdom, many professions now allow firms to be publicly listed companies, often with LLPs within the corporate group.

Many larger and international firms have a network of associated entities and undertakings. These can range from a 'one-firm' structure with centralised management and global profit sharing, where everyone stands (or falls) together, to a loose franchise-style arrangement between separately managed businesses, often with little legal connection other than shared branding and a set of 'club rules'.

For simplicity, this chapter assumes that the departing partner is a member of a UK LLP, although key differences for partners of a general partnership will be highlighted. The term 'partner' is adopted for both throughout for simplicity.

(b) Default regime

A simple framework of default rules applies to LLPs.[1] While the key components of the LLP and members' relationships are addressed, the default rules are not sophisticated enough to govern a modern professional firm.

LLP default rules

- Capital and profits shared equally.
- All members involved in management.
- Unrestricted access to LLP books and records for all members.
- Duty to account to LLP for unauthorised separate profits.
- Majority decision making, but change of business requires unanimity and no power to expel by majority.

Mercifully, the applicability of the default regime is subject to contrary agreement between the members and the LLP in an LLP agreement. Well-prepared firms ensure that their written agreement includes a full suite of exit-related provisions.

(c) Key LLP agreement exit provisions

From the firm's perspective, the inclusion of the following clauses will be vital.

Voluntary retirement: There must be power for members to give notice to retire voluntarily. A well-drafted provision will clearly specify how and to whom notice should be given (and align with the notices provision which is usually included as boilerplate).

There is no typical notice period, as firms have different attitudes to

"The applicability of the default regime is subject to contrary agreement between the members and the LLP in an LLP agreement. Well-prepared firms ensure that their written agreement includes a full suite of exit-related provisions."

managing tensions in this period. A longer period may allow for an orderly handover, enable the firm to cement relationships with clients and prevent a new firm from benefiting from the departing partner's contribution; but the departing partner will continue to earn profit share during the notice period.

Professional firm notice periods tend to range from three months to one year, with six or nine months probably being most common. Sometimes a distinction is drawn so that fixed share or junior equity partners have a shorter notice period.

The firm should have the power to shorten the notice period unilaterally to enable it to manage the timing of partner exits. To give partners a degree of financial certainty, this is usually coupled with the requirement that profit share for the full notice period (or an equivalent other payment) is still paid. This decision-making power would ideally be vested in a managing partner or board, rather than the full partner body, as the firm may need to move nimbly when negotiating exit terms.

Expulsion for cause: Firms should always have the power to expel partners for cause, to ensure that the firm is not saddled with an undesirable partner.

Causes should include:

- material breach of the agreement (and firm policies/procedures);
- criminal conviction;
- professional misconduct;
- loss of regulatory permissions;
- bankruptcy; and
- failure to perform usual duties for a prolonged period (eg, nine or 12 months).

It is in the firm's interests if the power to determine whether or not an expulsion event has occurred is vested in the firm (eg, in the managing partner or management committee).

Expulsion without cause: Market practice has evolved over the past 20 years and most firms now include a power to expel or remove without cause in their LLP agreements. This provides flexibility for firms to manage partners, and the composition of the partner body as a whole, without needing to provide compelling evidence of 'bad' behaviour. That said, the principles of natural justice mean that in practice, partners who are to be the subject of a removal vote are usually told the reasons for the proposed vote and given the opportunity to present their case (see further below).

The decision to remove a partner without cause is usually considered so fundamental that it is reserved to the partner body. Occasionally, this power is vested in management; but typically only in larger firms or those firms with a more 'corporate' structure that vest significant powers in a central management function. This approach is also prevalent in the accountancy sector.

The line between no-cause expulsion and voluntary retirement often becomes blurred – for example, when a firm wishes to expel a partner, but instead encourages him or her to give notice to retire, to avoid the embarrassment of being subjected to a formal decision about the proposed expulsion.

Other exit provisions: Most well-drafted LLP agreements also include the following retirement-related provisions. Each is worthy of a full chapter in its own right, but is briefly summarised below.

Table 1. Exit provisions

Suspension	To distance a partner from the business, staff and clients while serious performance or conduct issues are investigated.
Garden leave	If a partner is joining a competitor, this enables the firm to separate a partner from his or her clients and team, and gives the firm an opportunity to institutionalise the departing partner's client relationships. The partner continues to be subject to his or her duties as a partner and is therefore paid. Gardening leave must be for a reasonable period of time.
Restrictive covenants	These tend to cover non-compete and non-solicitation of staff and clients. Restrictions must be no more than are reasonable to protect the firm's legitimate business interests. Current market practice is for post-exit restrictions to endure for one to two years after the retirement date (usually reduced by whatever period has been served on garden leave).
Delayed repayment of current and capital account balances	Delayed repayment mitigates the impact of partner retirements on the firm's cash flow. The threat of withheld instalments also serves as an incentive for departing partners to comply with their post-exit restrictions.

It may be sensible to include requirements that partners must:

- notify the firm if they become aware that other partners are considering leaving;
- inform prospective firms of covenants that apply to them; and
- certify compliance with the agreement on demand.

(d) Less common provisions relating to retirement

Mandatory retirement age: A mandatory retirement age is discrimination on the grounds of age – one of many protected characteristics under the Equality Act 2010. This will be unlawful if it is not a proportionate means of achieving a legitimate business aim.

Many firms have now moved away from a mandatory retirement age. This appears to be in part to mitigate the risk of claims of age discrimination, whether justified or not, by disgruntled partners and former partners (the threats of uncapped damages and a public forum being useful weapons in a departing partner's armoury). Further, many firms conclude that performance and contribution are the only appropriate criteria to apply when making decisions about the composition of the firm.

The Association of Partnership Practitioners has collated data through periodic surveys to identify trends for professional firms.[2]

Figure 1. Percentage of firms using a mandatory retirement age

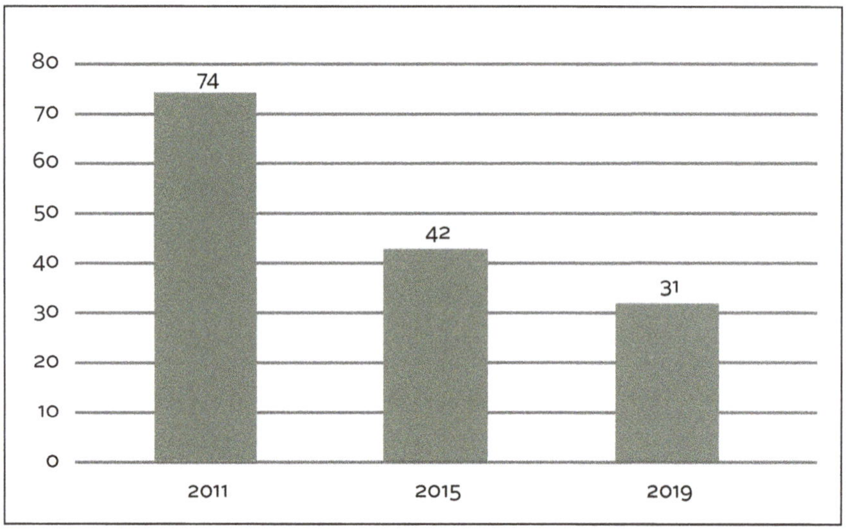

Figure 2. Mandatory retirement age 2011–2019

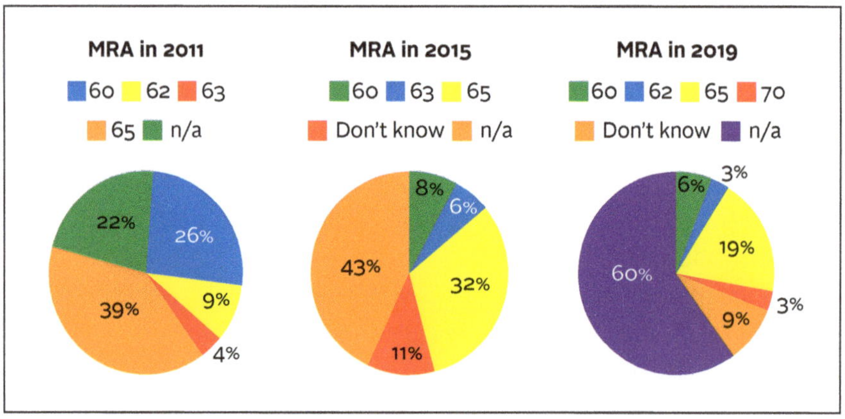

'Waiting room' provision: Some agreements include a 'waiting room' provision to prevent a flurry of exits from destabilising the firm. This could be as a result of a coordinated team move to a competitor or simply a group of partners retiring simultaneously by coincidence. The waiting room is usually achieved by allowing only a small number of partners to leave within a specified period (and preventing others from doing so until later). The risk is that one or more partners would be prevented from leaving, which may have an impact on their contribution and possibly on the firm's culture.

"Many firms conclude that performance and contribution are the only appropriate criteria to apply when making decisions about the composition of the firm."

If included, the system to determine who is permitted to leave must be perceived as fair. Care will be needed to ensure that criteria are not discriminatory. The firm may also want to retain discretion to make exceptions – for example, to manage the departure of unwanted/rogue partners or on compassionate grounds, such as where a person is terminally ill. Given the sensitivity usually associated with exceptions, it may be desirable for the power to grant exceptions to be vested in management rather than the full partner body.

(e) Annuities

Annuities are now rare, having been a feature of the now almost extinct phenomenon where people served their entire careers at one firm. They can also be a barrier to capital events, such as mergers, as acquiring firms are reluctant to assume the liabilities; or lateral recruitment, as incoming partners are often asked to assume personal responsibility for these payments.

If a firm still operates an annuity system, care may be needed to ensure that the documentation does not allow bad leavers to receive the same benefits as good leavers. Where there is a distinction, the firm may need to exercise powers to expel rather than allow such partners to jump before they are pushed and therefore retain their entitlement to annuities.

(f) Conclusion

Firms need to ensure they have a well-drafted agreement in order to manage partner exits effectively.

The dangers of failing to execute properly the LLP agreement (or its amendments) or deeds of accession – which is more common than you would think...

- Confusion and uncertainty. Likely to be risky, disruptive and expensive.
- May weaken the LLP's negotiating position in a settlement discussion.
- Vital protections may not apply. Consequences could include disputes being publicly litigated rather than privately arbitrated and Section 994 of the Companies Act not being validly excluded (it must be done in writing), enabling an individual member to threaten to wind up the LLP for unfair prejudice.
- Embarrassing. Partners may lose confidence in the management team's ability to manage risks effectively. If known publicly, law firms may also lose clients' confidence in the firm's ability to manage legal risks.

3. Voluntary retirement

A partner's voluntary retirement may be expected or unexpected.

The stereotypical example of an expected retirement is a partner reaching the end of a long and successful career and choosing to stop working, although often partners then pursue part-time or voluntary roles after retirement, such as non-executive directorships or charity trusteeships. Expected retirements are usually well planned between the partner and the firm – or at least they should be.

In this section, unexpected retirement is treated as the position where a person leaves the firm unexpectedly and without an opportunity for specific advance planning – for example, leaving to join a competitor. Unexpected retirements need not spell disaster for the firm. A former partner could join a client or prospective client and become an ambassador for the firm.

3.1 Expected retirements

Succession planning discussions should be a regular occurrence for all firms. It would be dangerously narrow minded to assume that succession planning should be broached only with partners within a certain age bracket.

Key elements for the firm to consider when succession planning

- Keep strategy and strengths under constant review. Does the current and anticipated future composition of the partner body enable the firm to achieve its strategic objectives?
- Institutionalise client relationships.
- Consider the impact of exits on practice groups and teams.
- Identify potential future leadership candidates early and prepare them, and the team, for change.
- Don't overlook management responsibilities and don't just assume that the successor in the practice group will step into all of the departing partner's shoes.
- Assess both the short and long-term financial implications of the partner's exit (eg, review cash-flow impact, work in progress, debtors).
- For key partners such as founder partners or partners who have led the firm for a prolonged period, consider the impact of exits on the market and the firm's people, culture and clients. Good internal and external communications are likely to be critical to manage disquiet about the end of an era.

"Succession planning discussions should be a regular occurrence for all firms. It would be dangerously narrow minded to assume that succession planning should be broached only with partners within a certain age bracket."

(a) Soft landing

Firms may want to encourage partners to retire at a time that best suits the firm – for example, to avoid the risks which arise where several partners retire simultaneously and/or to ensure a regular 'turnover' of partners to create opportunities for rising stars.

A soft landing may commence before a partner retires from the partnership, with a reduced working arrangement and/or decrease in points (if that is how profits are shared).

Firms may offer retiring partners consultancy arrangements, which may involve greater flexibility and/or part-time working arrangements. Remuneration is sometimes linked to billings and/or client introductions, although care is needed not to incentivise outgoing partners to hold on to clients, rather than cement the relationships with the firm and continuing partners.

Soft landing can also entail a variation of the default provisions relating to capital and accrued profits – for example, repaying capital in monthly instalments to supplement income when profit share drops or is replaced by salary.

"There is also an increasing trend for new businesses to create a model which allows founders or key partners to continue to participate as passive investors after they have ceased to be actively involved."

(b) New business models
The concept of anti-embarrassment clauses, which enable a recently retired partner to share in the proceeds of a capital event such as the disposal of the business or a subsidiary business, is well recognised – although not all firms extend this potential benefit to former partners.

There is also an increasing trend for new businesses to create a model which allows founders or key partners to continue to participate as passive investors after they have ceased to be actively involved. In a company this is relatively straightforward, as partners may be permitted to retain shares. In a partnership or LLP, it is more complex, because profits cannot be shared with non-partners. If those individuals remain as partners, they can receive a profit share and agree contractually to have a much reduced role; but they are still partners or LLP members with the associated statutory, fiduciary and contractual duties (and in a general partnership, full exposure to the firm's debts).

An alternative is that the individual ceases to be a member and receives a payment from the firm. It would be dangerous for the firm to agree a fixed sum with no flexibility for annual profit and cash-flow variations, so this is often described as a percentage of profits. This requires a notional calculation of profits to establish what the former partner would have been entitled to if he or she were still a partner before deducting that sum as an expense in order to calculate actual profits. This approach also enables the heirs of a deceased partner to continue to benefit, in the same way that they would have done if company shares passed under a person's will.

While the attraction of these arrangements is clear for those founders, there is a risk that (as with annuities) if a significant proportion of profits is earmarked for former partners, this may have a detrimental impact on the firm's ability to recruit and retain the top talent and thus depress growth and profitability.

This might be less of a concern if all firms were structured this way and/or the professional practices world evolves to a point where it is less reliant on individual partners' practices. Technology may hold the key to this evolution. Ironically, it may also drive the introduction of these arrangements, given the significant capital expenditure needed from the current generation of partners to adopt technological advances.

3.2 Unexpected retirements
A firm faces a number of risks with an unexpected retirement. Why is the partner leaving? Where is he or she going? Will he or she try to take staff or clients? What will clients/staff/the market think?

Many of the same considerations apply as for an expected retirement, although within a different timeframe and usually with greater pressure. For example, successors will need to be identified, clients handed over and the team reassured. This is another reason why firms would be well advised to have ongoing succession plans permanently in place.

(a) Notice and garden leave

The notice period is likely to be invaluable to prepare the firm for the partner's exit. A firm may also decide to place a partner on garden leave, assuming that it has the power to do so. These powers allow the firm to prohibit interaction with clients and staff.

In practice, this may be difficult if the firm has ongoing responsibilities to clients which cannot immediately or sensibly be assumed by someone else. For regulated professionals, this is obviously a key consideration. A firm may be able to strike a sensible balance by restricting the partner to certain activities and prohibiting others.

(b) Investigations

It may be sensible or necessary to investigate the conduct of departing partners, in particular in the period leading up to their notice.

Those joining competitor firms may have shared confidential internal or client information to secure those roles. In many cases this is unlikely to involve malicious intent: hiring firms want to make informed decisions and many recruitment consultants issue 'standard' questionnaires requesting vast amounts of confidential information, such as billing and recovery figures, charge-out rates, clients' names, team members' names and so on. The provision of such information is highly likely to be a breach of the LLP agreement and regulatory obligations, and will therefore require a report to a regulatory authority.

If partners have liaised with one another to coordinate an exit and/or approached team members to encourage them to leave too, then that collusion is also a breach of their duties as partners at law and under the agreement.

A firm's investigation may seek to establish the extent, if any, to which a partner has or may have breached his or her duties to the firm. It may also enable the firm to take steps to prevent damage. For example, forensic IT analysis can reveal where partners have downloaded data onto external hard drives/USBs (assuming that the firm has not taken the precaution of disabling this function), printed out or copied unusually high volumes of material (sometimes at unusual times) and/or emailed data to personal email addresses. These actions will not necessarily represent a breach by a partner,

"If partners have liaised with one another to coordinate an exit and/or approached team members to encourage them to leave too, then that collusion is also a breach of their duties as partners at law and under the agreement."

but an informed firm will be in a position to consider the potential risks and engage with the partner to establish the rationale for his or her activities.

If the firm concludes that the partner has behaved improperly, it may put him or her on garden leave or consider taking some form of formal action (eg, claiming for damages). Even if not, the results of the investigation may improve the firm's negotiating position in a settlement discussion.

4. Involuntary retirement

As noted above, an involuntary retirement may result from the exercise of a power to remove for cause or without cause.

4.1 The importance of good process

Whenever a firm is exercising powers to remove, good process is vital. First, the firm must ensure that it is acting within the scope of its powers under the agreement (hence the importance of a well-drafted agreement). If the correct process is not followed, the firm may find that the attempts to remove a partner have been ineffective and the partner continues to serve as such (but on notice that the firm is trying to get rid of him or her).

Second, the firm should respect the principles of natural justice and ensure that the powers are not exercised for an improper motive or capriciously.

4.2 Reasons

A properly drafted power to remove without cause will not require a firm to give reasons. However, the firm will want to consider whether to give reasons for proposing the exercise of the power. The decision makers will want to know why the person's removal is proposed. The individual who is the subject of the decision will want the opportunity to put his or her case before the decision is made.

The reasons will be different in each case. It goes without saying that the reasons should be appropriate and lawful.

Backward-looking reasons will probably be strongly contested by a resistant partner. For example, if poor performance is cited, evidence of poor performance is needed from the firm and the partner will presumably also a table a body of contradictory evidence showing satisfactory performance, or equally poor or worse performance by others.

Firms may find that partners find it harder to argue against forward-looking reasons, such as non-alignment with the firm's future strategy.

Common procedural mistakes made by firms

- **Notice:** Failure to observe the correct period or to give notice in accordance with the specific notices provision (a clause which is often considered only to be 'boilerplate').
- **Grounds for expulsion:** Inadequate grounds or insufficient evidence to prove the grounds – it is common to find that the firm has not created written evidence of performance or disciplinary discussions.
- **Communication:** Care is needed to communicate properly and appropriately. Key messages should be confirmed (briefly) in writing to avoid uncertainty. Consider communications training to avoid errors which could undermine the whole process – for example, using language which implies that a decision was based on a protected characteristic such as age or gender.
- **Garden leave/suspension:** Restricting a partner's access to the premises or access to IT systems without the power to do so (or before having obtained the correct decision to do so). If a firm does not have this power, but perceives a partner to be a serious threat, it may take the view that it is (commercially) safer to act without appropriate powers.

5. The exit

All partner retirement processes will conclude in one of three ways:

- departure under the default terms (ie, usually as set out in the written agreement which varies the statutory default rules);
- a negotiated exit, usually with a deed of retirement which varies the default terms; or
- a big fight, culminating in an arbitration, tribunal or court proceeding.

The threat of a fight may precede a negotiated exit and/or be used to try to improve agreed exit terms.

5.1 Risks for the firm during the exit process

The key risks for the firm derive from the departing partner's weaponry. Probably the most dangerous departing partners are those who are prepared to have their bluff called and will pursue their grievance(s) as far as possible.

The firm can mitigate the risks of claims arising against the firm by being prepared and respecting its powers and due process, but often the firm's role in an unexpected exit tends to be reactive rather than proactive. There are some exceptions to this general principle where the firm takes steps against the partner(s) and/or the acquiring firm, such as on a team move or where the firm has discovered evidence of serious breach or misconduct. This might include injunctive action to try to prevent damage from occurring. Action could be taken against the departing partner(s) and possibly also recruitment agents and/or an acquiring firm, on the grounds of procuring a breach by the departing partner(s), conspiracy and/or breach of confidence. In the regulated sector, their conduct may constitute a regulatory breach – for example, if a firm has aggressively encouraged an incoming partner to disclose client confidential data in breach of the rules, knowing that disclosure would be a regulatory breach.

5.2 What allegations might be made against the firm?

A well-drafted written agreement limits the action that can be taken by a partner. For example, Section 994 of the Companies Act 2006 will be excluded to prevent partners from bringing an unfair prejudice action.

The agreement will almost always also require the resolution of disputes in a private forum, such as through mediation or arbitration (often one, then the other). This enables the firm to manage potentially embarrassing and distracting disputes privately, and therefore neutralises an aggrieved partner's threat to embarrass the firm publicly.

"Partners do not enjoy the same level of statutory protections as employees, but they are protected from unlawful discrimination, harassment and victimisation."

A commonly observed exception to this in practice is the threat of a discrimination claim. Partners do not enjoy the same level of statutory protections as employees, but they are protected from unlawful discrimination, harassment and victimisation. A discrimination claim will be heard in the Employment Tribunal, circumnavigating an arbitration provision, and can give rise to potentially uncapped damages. Since 2014 it has also been clear that LLP members enjoy some additional protections as 'workers'.[3] The most significant of these is the potentially uncapped compensation if it is found that the LLP member suffered an unlawful detriment for whistleblowing.

The firm should try to avoid giving a departing partner an opportunity to assert these claims successfully. Ideally, it will have a full body of evidence supporting the legitimate reasons for the partner's exit, such as a string of written poor performance reviews, despite offering support including mentoring and coaching. It should also work hard to foster a culture which does not tolerate inappropriate behaviours, to mitigate the risk that individual partners might make inappropriate comments based on individuals' personal (legally protected) characteristics. For an aggrieved departing partner, a 'smoking gun' email recording those inappropriate views – for example, an email exchange between two partners about how a female partner is 'not one of the boys' or an older partner is 'not as young as s/he was' –

will be very powerful. A subject access request under data protection laws could reveal such communications with little expense or effort on the part of the departing partner. An aggrieved partner may also cite written provisions, such as mandatory retirement age provisions, or established working practices, such as partners being encouraged to leave at a certain age, as evidence of unlawful discrimination on the grounds of age.

In many cases, such grievances will settle before reaching an arbitration or tribunal; but the firm may find that it must make substantial concessions in a negotiation if faced with a strong claim and a determined partner.

On this note, disproportionate expense is often cited as a barrier to individuals bringing claims and/or being prepared to pursue them fully (especially in professional services disputes, where the sums at stake tend to be lower than in financial services businesses). Firms should not rely too heavily on this. This is increasingly less relevant, as more flexible costs options are offered by law firms and litigation funding is more readily available. Also, legal expenses of this nature are often covered by individuals' home insurance.

5.3 A negotiated settlement

Negotiated settlements are the most common outcomes for firms and their departing partners.

A firm can offer a departing partner a number of concessions in order to achieve a mutually agreed settlement.

Concessions that firms may consider

- Shorter notice period: To allow the partner to join his or her new firm or begin his or her next project within the desired timeframe. This may also enable the partner to harness overlap relief more effectively and achieve tax savings. Client service and regulatory implications will need to be carefully considered.
- Accelerated payment of capital and/or accrued and undistributed profits: If cash flow permits, this may alleviate the partner's personal financial position and acknowledge the counterparty risk that former partners take on their former firms. Firms may resist early repayment if the threat of set-off/withholding is intended to encourage adherence to post-exit covenants.
- Release of tax reserves: This is rare, but may be welcome for the same reasons as noted immediately above.
- More money: It is rare for a firm to increase a partner's profit

share for his or her final year, but it can happen. However, it is common for the firm and partner to agree a final sum for the final year's profit share based on management accounts and/or projections if the departure date is not a year-end, so that the firm and partner do not have to delay conclusion of the matter until after the year-end accounts have been approved.

- Waiver of restrictive covenants: Either a complete waiver or a partial waver. Partial waivers may be palatable to the firm if the departing partner had a niche practice which the firm cannot or does not wish to continue. Waivers also respect the commercial reality that clients may not react well to a suggestion that they cannot freely choose who to instruct.
- Team moves: If the departure of one or more partners creates a huge hole in one of the firm's practice areas, the firm can try to recruit or promote to plug that gap. However, the firm may recognise that these efforts would be insufficient, and could either waive covenants to allow the rest of the team to leave as well or enter into discussions with the partner/acquiring firm to agree a demerger of that group. This would reduce/eliminate the excess overheads and may pass risk to the acquiring firm – for example, if there is a transfer of undertakings of the team's employees and/or if the acquiring firm serves as a successor practice for professional indemnity purposes.
- Transfer of mobile phone number: This may be a risk if the firm wishes to constrain clients' ability to make contact with a former partner in the future; but in view of the widespread adoption of social media – in particular, LinkedIn and Twitter – this is unlikely to achieve that objective.
- Outplacement support: To enable partners to transition to a future role. This is most common where the exit is at the firm's instigation.
- Budget for legal expenses: A capped sum to review and advise on settlement documentation.
- Extended notice period: This is unusual, but in exceptional circumstances may be welcome – for example, if a partner wants existing life insurance or health insurance cover to continue, or wants to continue to use the firm's email address or premises while securing his or her next role.

5.4 Avoid the temptation to be vindictive

While it is reasonable to take steps which mitigate risks to the firm, little is achieved by making the departure process as difficult as possible for a departing partner just for the sake of it. Partnerships and LLPs are usually owner-managed businesses where the partners often forge strong bonds and lifelong friendships. This is one of their great strengths as a business form. However, like family disputes, there can be an emotional element to partner exits – even those that are agreed and/or long-planned.

It would be short-sighted for a firm to act vindictively or discourteously in its dealings with a departing partner, even where the partner has behaved poorly. This is unlikely to have a positive impact on the firm's culture because the firm's leadership, who will invariably be at the centre of exit negotiations, must embody its culture and values.

Former partners – even those who do not retire voluntarily – are often a firm's greatest ambassadors, but only if they feel that they have been treated fairly and reasonably. The commercial rationale for being polite and sensible is clear.

In short, when handling partner retirements, it is vital for the firm to be prepared, be right and be nice.

Notes

1 Limited Liability Partnerships Regulations 2001, Sections 7 and 8. These are very similar to the default regime applicable to general partnerships under the Partnership Act 1890 (at Sections 24 and 25).

2 Data collected in surveys conducted by the Association of Partnership Practitioners in 2011, 2015 (47 respondent firms) and 2019 (36 respondent firms).

3 See the 2014 Supreme Court decision in *Clyde & Co LLP v Bates van Winkelhof*. Lady Hale in that decision made it clear that the decision could not extend to partners of general partnerships.

II. Legal issues from the individual partner's point of view

Ivor Adair
Caroline Field
Fox & Partners

Partners may retire at the end of their career as part of a planned consensual departure or on terms provided for in the partnership agreement.

As partners move to the end of their career, diverging expectations of the firm and individual can create conflict. Partners are often pushed into processes they had not anticipated – for example, performance management resulting in points reduction or de-equitisation. While uncommon in the professional services sector, where reputations are carefully guarded, there may be litigation in the courts or employment tribunal, or arbitration (a private forum). This chapter considers the two broad categories of retirement – voluntary and involuntary – from the partner's perspective.

1. Objectives

For most professional partners, work is a huge part of life. When faced with a potential change in that context, objectivity often goes out of the window. Our top tip to a partner facing retirement is always to keep your own objectives firmly in mind and acknowledge the (legitimate) objectives of the firm. Share these at an early stage with family and professional advisers, who can help to keep you on track. Regularly re-evaluate. An experienced adviser can tell you how your particular standpoint will be received and assist you with strategies to meet your objectives.

Even a party taken by surprise will quickly realise that there is little sense in staying somewhere he or she is not wanted or, from the firm's point of view, trying to keep someone who has disengaged.

A partner will typically want to leave on generous terms, possibly in a manner and on terms which enable him or her to work unimpeded elsewhere. The firm will want to avoid litigation and protect the business. Firms often prefer to avoid referring forced retirement to a vote, which reflects management shortcomings and can be unsettling to other partners or damaging in the wider context of what is going on at the firm (eg, if a merger is contemplated).

All of these factors, coupled with the constraints on the operation of involuntary processes, mean that there is usually opportunity for a negotiated outcome.

2. Considerations for retiring partners negotiating their exit

The starting point will always be a careful review of the partnership or LLP deed and related documentation. A proper evaluation of objectives, priorities, risks (legal, financial and reputational), potential claims, how advice will be funded, the personalities of key individuals within the partnership and the likely posture that the firm will adopt in any negotiation will be important. Here is a checklist of issues to consider:

- How much notice must the partner give to the firm of his or her intention to leave?
- Is there a power of compulsory retirement or expulsion? In what circumstances may such power be exercised?
- Are there provisions which require age-related action, such as role review meetings or a mandatory retirement age? Such provisions are potentially discriminatory under the Equality Act 2010, unless they can be objectively justified.
- What procedure must the firm follow to effect an involuntary retirement? Who has the power to do so? Is it reserved to a vote of the partners? Are all partners entitled to vote? What majority is required? Is there a right of appeal?
- Is the firm entitled to put the partner on garden leave/suspend the partner? In the absence of an express right in the partnership agreement, firms may be unable to instruct a partner to stay away pending investigation or during notice (voluntary or involuntary). Where available, suspension is common pending investigation in the context of expulsion. The firm is likely to take the view that disgruntled partners damage morale. In the context of voluntary departures, a firm may endeavour to protect client relationships. To avoid challenge, members and partners should expect profit share and other benefits to continue for the duration.

- Is there a 'waiting room' provision which prevents a certain number of partners from leaving the firm within a specified period?
- What are the financial entitlements linked to the options for exit? Most partnership agreements have extensive provisions addressing the entitlements of a partner on retirement. In the absence of agreement, valuation of a partner's share or interest is likely to be contentious and complex, and may involve valuation of goodwill. Most professional service firm models now operate on the basis that you don't pay for goodwill on your way in and are not entitled to a share on your way out. Key considerations include what happens to a partner's current account balance, profit share for open financial years, capital account and tax reserve. Other considerations include the following:
  - What happens to membership of any benefit schemes (eg, medical insurance, life insurance) on retirement?
  - Is there a contractual right of set-off against sums owed by the partner to the firm (eg, excess drawings)?
  - Is there any conditionality to payments or claw-back provisions which could require the partner to repay sums to the firm?

"Many firms operate as if management information were confidential. If the agreement does not expressly provide otherwise, the default regimes give members the right to access 'books' at any time."

- Are appropriate indemnities and insurance provisions set out in the partnership agreement in respect of existing and future liabilities of the partnership? In a traditional partnership, subject to contrary agreement, a partner remains liable after retirement for debts and liabilities incurred by the partnership when he or she was a partner.
- Has the partner given personal guarantees in respect of partnership loans, leases or other liabilities? When will they be released?
- Is there an express duty of good faith between partners and, in the context of an LLP, between members and the LLP? Even if there is no express duty, in traditional partnerships, partners owe each other a duty of utmost good faith. Some consequences of the duty were codified in the Partnership Act 1890. While there is no general application of partnership law to LLPs, members of an LLP are also likely to owe fiduciary duties to the firm as its agent. Generally, the duties can be summarised as follows (and may be set out in the agreement):
  - to act in the best interests and promote the business of the firm;
  - to avoid conflict between their own interests and the interests of the firm – this would include competing in business with the firm, and soliciting clients or employees of the firm for a competitor business which they will be joining;
  - not to use their position as partners of the firm, or use information learned or opportunities acquired by them in that capacity, for personal advantage; and
  - to make full and fair disclosure of all information which they obtain which is material to the business. The default regimes also include disclosure obligations, if not excluded or varied.
- Are there post-retirement restrictive covenants? Unless the agreement provides otherwise, partners will be free to move on unrestricted. There may be some limited constraint on traditional partners soliciting existing clients of their former firm. Partnership agreements now often contain extensive restrictions purporting to protect legitimate business interests.
- Are there ongoing duties of confidentiality?
- What announcements will the firm and the partner wish to make, externally and internally? Actual notice to clients of a traditional partnership (who are entitled to treat all apparent members of the firm as constituted at the time of their engagement as still being partners) will be required. Ideally, suppliers and third parties should also be notified of any changes, to ensure that the partner has no liability for the firm's post-retirement dealings. Section 37 of the Partnership Act enables partners to publicise their retirement. However, the interrelationship of this provision with partners' fiduciary duties

must be given careful consideration. The best course is usually to agree the wording and timing of any announcement with the firm.

- Has the partner experienced discrimination and or whistleblowing victimisation? Are there viable employment tribunal claims?
- If the firm is an LLP, does the LLP agreement exclude the right to claim unfair prejudice under Section 994 of the Companies Act 2006?
- Are disputes resolved by arbitration or mediation or in the courts?
- Does the partner have access to internal documents and information? Many firms operate as if management information were confidential. If the agreement does not expressly provide otherwise, the default regimes give members the right to access 'books' at any time and oblige each partner to render true accounts and full information of all things affecting the partnership to any member or his or her legal representative.

3. The default regime – the Partnership Act 1890 and Limited Liability Partnership Act 2000

The rights and duties of partners and members of an LLP are governed by the agreement between them. The provisions of the LLP Act and the default provisions set out in the Limited Liability Partnerships Regulations 2001 (in the case of an incorporated LLP) and the Partnership Act (in the case of general partnerships) will be deemed to apply in the absence of agreement; in certain limited respects, the default provisions are mandatory.

The default regimes will be relevant if matters covered by the default rules are not clearly expressed in the agreements between partners.

The most significant aspect of the default regimes in this context is that, in the absence of agreement between partners or members, an individual cannot be expelled or compulsorily retired by other partners or members. Indeed, in a general partnership, a partner cannot voluntarily retire without bringing about the potential dissolution and subsequent winding up of the partnership, unless he or she has the consent of all the other partners or the partnership agreement provides for it. In the absence of contrary agreement, the main options will be dissolving the partnership/winding up the LLP and subsequently reforming the firm or reaching agreement on terms which strongly favour the departing partner.

4. The exit routes

Given the grave consequences of the default regimes, most LLP and partnership agreements expressly address routes to exit.

"Understanding partners' retirement aspirations enables the firm to provide tailored support, plan for transfer of knowledge and experience to future leaders and facilitate the transfer of client relationships."

4.1 Voluntary

Increasingly, firms are recognising the importance of proactive succession planning. While it is essential for any successful firm to free up equity to incentivise rising stars, the value of maintaining relationships with experienced partners with significant connections and reputations should not be underestimated. This is not an easy dynamic to manage.

Some larger firms approach retirement in a more formal way by building in role review meetings at which specific criteria are addressed. Participation may, in turn, be part of the criteria for enhanced benefits on departure, often referred to as a 'soft landing'.

Planned consensual departure is by far the best way for a partner to leave a firm. This may be pursuant to voluntary retirement terms of the written agreement by giving reasonable notice to the other partners. Alternatively, it may be by way of separately negotiated agreement.

Most firms welcome a dialogue with partners considering retirement. Understanding partners' retirement aspirations enables the firm to provide tailored support, plan for transfer of knowledge and experience to future leaders and facilitate the transfer of client relationships; it may also open the door to retention of a partner's experience in a non-partner role. A shock announcement may make the firm wary of a partner's future plans.

4.2 Involuntary

Unless there is a reason to remove a partner quickly, firms often try 'softer' options to encourage partners towards retirement if they feel that it is time for them to move on. Coaching, performance management and informal discussions are options. These may be challenged if not managed appropriately by the firm and in accordance with any agreement. The involuntary mechanisms loom in the background if things don't improve.

Termination provisions in partnership agreements are typically divided into two separate categories: expulsion and compulsory retirement.

(a) Expulsion

Expulsion (usually recognised as the 'fault-based' or 'for cause' power) is usually effective immediately and reserved for serious misbehaviour akin to gross misconduct. The provision usually prescribes the circumstances in which a partner can be removed from the firm. Examples include where a partner is convicted of a criminal offence, becomes bankrupt, commits persistent breaches of the LLP agreement or is guilty of conduct likely to have a material adverse effect on the business.

(b) Compulsory retirement

Compulsory retirement is usually on notice and is not predicated on a particular ground being made out. Historically, this power was referred to as a 'without cause' or 'no-fault' power. Such a categorisation may not now be sound, given developments in the law relating to contractual discretion.

Draconian involuntary powers are construed strictly against the firm.

Even where the express rights to remove a partner are available theoretically, the law imposes equitable constraints on discretionary decision-making powers.

Good faith: Fiduciary duties between partners in a general partnership require partners to exercise discretion in good faith, acting honestly, in the best interests of the partnership and with regard to the purpose of the decision. The prevailing view in relation to LLPs is that the court is likely to imply obligations of good faith into discretionary decision making in relation to powers of expulsion or compulsory retirement.

Process and outcome limitations: In *Braganza v BP Shipping Ltd* the Supreme Court confirmed that contractual terms giving one party the power to exercise a discretion or form an opinion as to relevant facts which may adversely affect the interests of the other party must not be exercised in a way which is arbitrary, capricious or irrational. Assessment is by reference to the test used in the judicial review of the decision of a public body.

The test allows the court to overturn the conclusion reached by a decision maker where:

- the decision maker has:
  - taken into account matters which he or she ought not to have taken into account; or
  - conversely, refused or neglected to take into account matters which he or she ought to have taken into account; or
- the decision is so unreasonable that no reasonable authority could ever have come to it.

The majority of the Supreme Court distinguished the employment context justifying more rigorous scrutiny of an employer's decision and application of both limbs.

A contractual discretion is to be distinguished from a simple decision of whether to exercise an absolute contractual right. The protection is not deemed necessary if the contract confers a discretion which is exercisable only if certain conditions are met (eg, most expulsion provisions). The court will decide, as a matter of fact, whether those conditions have been met.

Subsequent case law has left the position outside an employment context far from clear.

An LLP member faced with forced retirement without rhyme or reason has no unfair dismissal rights and no right of repudiation (which offer protection to an employee). In circumstances where the court seeks to ensure that exercise of discretion is not abused, it may confer a degree of protection on members.

Natural justice to the rescue: Even if the first limb of *Braganza* does not apply, natural justice is likely to demand that members and partners know the charges against them and have an opportunity to set out their defence in circumstances where there is an exercise of discretion. If retirement is being forced under compulsory retirement provisions, a member should be given an opportunity to state his or her case.

(c) What are the implied duties likely to mean for partners facing compulsory retirement?

- Decision makers must act honestly in the best interests of partnership and not for an ulterior motive.
- A partner must be treated fairly by being:
  - informed of complaints or concerns in sufficient detail to enable a response. If a procedure is set out, it should be observed scrupulously; and
  - given the opportunity to respond to the substance of concerns and whether substantiated concerns justify the proposed action;
- If the *Braganza* duty is applied, decision makers must focus on the purpose of the discretion. The firm will need to be satisfied and, in turn, satisfy the retiring partner or a court/arbitrator that relevant factors were taken into account and irrelevant factors disregarded.

In the context of expulsion, refusing to allow a partner to put forward his or her position may indicate bad faith.

5. Challenging expulsion/compulsory retirement and tactical considerations for partners

Law firms are unlikely to relish their decision making being scrutinised or taken out of their control. The partner will view an involuntary process (potentially including a members' vote) as highly undesirable. A negotiated settlement is likely to be in all parties' interests.

Broadly, an attack on expulsion or compulsory retirement may be based on one or more of the following:

- unlawful exercise of expulsion powers, including the following:
  - the ground is not made out (in expulsion cases or where there is a stated basis for compulsory retirement);
  - the proper procedure, either express or implied pursuant to the *Braganza* duty and principles of natural justice, was not followed; or
  - bad faith or an ulterior/improper motive; or
- employment tribunal claims, including discrimination or whistleblowing.

5.1 Unlawful exercise of the retirement powers

While both parties rarely want a public dispute, any pre-action challenge must be managed carefully in accordance with objectives. It is not wise to call the firm's bluff in reliance on an assumed preference not to go to a partner vote, unless the partner is willing to see the process through. Raising concerns in the interests of the firm and asking for an opportunity to explain to the right audience how the decision makers have got it wrong may form part of a strategy to improve your position. It will be important to consider the mechanics of the power carefully, both for the purpose of mounting a challenge and to understand the relevant timescales for doing so.

Some of the matters a partner might want to raise may include the following:

- Are the facts relied upon made out? Has a fair investigation been undertaken?
- Is there any evidence of an agenda in relation to his or her removal? Highlight any evidence of pre-determination or canvassing of support and make clear, if appropriate, that the decision is for the partners.
- Outline any shortcomings in the process – has any express procedure been followed? Has the basis for the proposed retirement been outlined in sufficient detail (or at all) to the partner? Has the rationale for any proposed action and documentation been prepared/circulated to decision makers? Was there an opportunity to respond as to the substantive concerns and sanction? If the matter is reserved to a vote of the partners, was there an opportunity to speak to the partnership?

"If there is any doubt, the partner should carefully examine the facts informing his or her status in order to ascertain whether enhanced employment rights are available. The label of 'partner' does not always accord with the true status of the relationship."

- Highlight the firm's duties and the purpose of any discretionary decision-making power (eg, to ensure that the best interests of the firm are served by retaining those who contribute to the firm and meet criteria for partnership). Have the right matters been taken into account? Is there a framework for assessing partner performance that focuses on success indicators? Highlight strengths in client relationships, collaboration, people development and contribution to the firm's overall profitability, and shift the focus away from individual billings if that is the issue.
- Would a comparative exercise involving other members of the firm result in the partner's selection when judged against criteria reflecting the values of the firm? Was an opportunity given for improvement and has the firm kept its side of the bargain?
- Does the conduct of the process impugn the values of the firm? What message does it give to new/progressing partners? What other consequences arise from the firm's actions – does it raise questions for other partners in a national practice or specific discipline that may have been overlooked?
- Is further information required? Outline the partner's rights to documents and information regarding the process.
- Express dismay about any indiscretion/insensitivity of the firm after many years of loyal service (if that is the case) and highlight the partner's contribution. Bear in mind that the document may be circulated to a wider audience in due course.
- It is likely to be sensible for the partner to remain vague about his or her next steps.

If it is established that an expulsion or compulsory retirement was invalid, the partner will remain a partner and will be entitled to be restored to the position that he or she would have been in had he or she not been invalidly expelled or retired. There may even be scope for an application for an injunction to restrain the breach of contract should a retirement notice be served. In reality, a partner is unlikely to return to the partnership; but the value of any exit package may be significantly improved.

5.2 Employment tribunal rights

Partners do not qualify for most statutory employment protection rights, such as unfair dismissal. Traditional partners and LLP members are protected by the discrimination legislation. Members of an LLP are likely to fall within the statutory definition of a 'worker' and will therefore be entitled to whistleblowing protection.

If there is any doubt, the partner should carefully examine the facts informing his or her status in order to ascertain whether enhanced employment rights are available. The label of 'partner' does not always accord with the true status of the relationship. Partnership and employment are mutually exclusive; an individual cannot be a member of an LLP and be employed by it in any circumstances.

Discrimination and whistleblowing allegations are invariably sensitive, difficult to prove and hard to resolve. Close bonds between partners forged by law and partnership business culture, and the regulated environment in which professional service firms operate, can result in heightened emotional reactions to such claims. Claims are often perceived by firms as an attempt to add pressure or a bargaining chip to secure a more financially favourable exit from the partnership. This can result in the issues raised by the partner not being taken sufficiently seriously and provoke alienation of the retiring partner. This, in turn, can escalate matters and introduce litigation and reputational risks. Partners should be prepared to substantiate allegations.

Key benefits include the following:

- Subject to causation and duties to mitigate, the compensation for financial losses is uncapped. If the firm's actions contribute to difficulties for the partner in securing a new role, there may be a sustainable claim for considerable financial losses, along with the possibility of claims for injury to feelings or personal injury.
- Claims can be pursued, in the absence of unreasonable conduct, without a risk of liability for the firm's costs.
- A final hearing of any claims is likely to be heard in public and decisions of employment tribunal cases in England, Wales and Scotland are published on the website of Her Majesty's Courts & Tribunals Service. The risk of reputational damage is significant.
- There may be regulatory implications for the partnership and/or individual partners where malpractice is exposed in the course of investigating whistleblowing complaints.
- A partner may be personally liable as agent under the Equality Act, those acts potentially binding the firm.

The claims most likely to be relevant in this context are discussed further below.

(a) Discrimination

There are nine protected characteristics enjoyed by partners under the Equality Act. It is unlawful to discriminate against a partner by treating him or her less favourably because of any of the protected characteristics. Age and disability may be particularly relevant in the context of the retirement of older partners. Retirement ages have

"If the firm's actions contribute to difficulties for the partner in securing a new role, there may be a sustainable claim for considerable financial losses, along with the possibility of claims for injury to feelings or personal injury."

been retained by many professional services firms. Stereotyping (eg, that younger partners are more productive or amenable to change) or prejudicial assumptions may apparently motivate expulsion or compulsory retirement. Key areas where partners may suffer detrimental treatment because of age and disability discrimination include:

- performance management;
- access to progression opportunities;
- points allocation (if this is how profit is shared) or bonuses;
- involuntary retirement processes; and
- other detriments focused on bringing about retirement.

The threshold for what constitutes a detriment is low. It does not necessitate physical or financial consequences. Demotion, reduction of profit share or a bad reference after leaving the partnership would constitute detrimental treatment.

A further claim (known as victimisation) can be made where, broadly, a partner is subjected to a detriment because he or she has done or is believed to have done a 'protected act'. A protected act includes alleging that the respondent or another person has contravened the Equality Act. False statements in bad faith will not be protected. It is not uncommon for arguable but nonetheless shaky discrimination allegations, handled poorly by a firm, to evolve into a strong victimisation tribunal claim. There is also scope for separate harassment allegations under the Equality Act by a partner who personally feels humiliated, keeping in mind that the definition includes the scenario where the violations had an effect even if they did not have that purpose.

Age discrimination: The basic starting point is for the partner to demonstrate that he or she has been treated 'less favourably' than a real or hypothetical comparator. A partner who is affected by a mandatory retirement age, or who is unexpectedly approached and asked to leave the partnership following negative comments regarding his or her performance or behaviour when younger partners with similar performance or behaviour have not, may have grounds for a complaint of age discrimination.

Given the requirement to establish that the treatment is 'because of' a protected characteristic, the subjective thought processes of key decision makers are a central issue in proving discrimination. The building blocks of the claim will often involve establishing facts from which age discrimination could be inferred. Evidence may include

"Age discrimination is capable of being objectively justified if it can be established that discriminatory action was a proportionate means of achieving a legitimate aim."

evasively answered questions, false explanations, breaches of relevant codes of practice or ageist remarks. If the partner can show a *prima facie* case by proving facts from which it could be inferred that discrimination has taken place, the burden of proof shifts to the respondent firm to show that it did not discriminate.

Even if the partner proves age discrimination, his or her claim will not necessarily succeed. Age discrimination is capable of being objectively justified if it can be established that discriminatory action was a proportionate means of achieving a legitimate aim. In the context of direct age discrimination, the legitimate aim must be of a public interest nature. In considering compulsory retirement of a partner at 65 in accordance with the partnership agreement, the Supreme Court recognised 'inter-generational fairness' and preserving the 'dignity' of older workers by avoiding unseemly debates about capacity to be legitimate aims. However, the question will still be: what is legitimate in the particular circumstances? For example, if the firm already has sophisticated performance management measures in place, it may not be legitimate to avoid them for retiring partners. The means chosen by the firm will also be scrutinised to see whether they meet the objective or whether other less discriminatory measures could be deployed.

The concept of legitimate aims, which necessitates the consideration of the issues before any instance of discrimination raised by the partner, may prove challenging for firms. The firm must balance the needs of the business against the discriminatory effect. A partner considering claims for age discrimination may apply some pressure on the firm by questioning its aims, why they are in the public interest, evidence to support the alleged problems addressed by the aims and the firm's consideration of other less discriminatory means. This may be done by raising a grievance or by asking questions as to whether the firm agrees with the description of the treatment and how it is justified.

Disability discrimination: The Equality Act provides protection for partners who are disabled, which means establishing that they have a physical or mental impairment that has a substantial and long-term adverse effect on their ability to carry out normal day-to-day activities.

In the context of retirement, common issues include allegations that the partner has suffered unjustified unfavourable treatment because of something arising in consequence of his or her disability (eg, a period of sick leave) or a failure to make reasonable adjustments. Partners suffering from health problems (which may also result in behavioural change) can face criticisms of erratic or poor performance or that they are incapable.

"How candid and forthcoming the partner is about his or her health and work situation can therefore have a bearing on the strength of claims and the posture the firm may adopt in response to allegations of discrimination."

It is often prudent for the partner to disclose the disability in writing, articulate what it is about the particular set-up at the firm that makes it difficult for him or her to do his or her job, and request adjustments.

How candid and forthcoming the partner is about his or her health and work situation can therefore have a bearing on the strength of claims and the posture the firm may adopt in response to allegations of discrimination. Whether adjustments (eg, altering duties, working hours or modifying procedures) are required will depend on whether they are objectively reasonable.

(b) Whistleblowing

Whistleblowing protection is extended to 'workers' and therefore most LLP members. Whistleblowing is the oral or written disclosure of information to the firm, which in the reasonable belief of the partner relates to wrongdoing that has taken place, is taking place or is likely to take place, where the disclosure is made in the public interest (a 'protected disclosure').

Workers have the right not to be subjected to any detriment on the grounds that they have made a 'protected disclosure'. Typical challenges to a whistleblowing claim include the following:

- The disclosure is a mere allegation that does not convey facts and is therefore not a disclosure of 'information'. However, the partner may be able to establish there is sufficient factual content and specifics to constitute information.
- The partner's belief was not reasonably held. However, it does not matter if the belief subsequently turns out to be wrong, provided that the partner subjectively believes that wrongdoing has taken place, is taking place or is likely to take place, and the employment tribunal considers that view to be objectively reasonable.
- The disclosure was not made 'in the public interest'. Relevant factors will include:
  - the numbers in the group whose interests the disclosure served;
  - the nature and the extent to which such interests are affected by the wrongdoing;
  - the nature of the alleged wrongdoing; and
  - the identity of the alleged wrongdoer.

The main battleground in whistleblowing claims is usually causation. Where the protected disclosure has more than a trivial influence on the detrimental treatment of the partner, causation will be established.

"The main battleground in whistleblowing claims is usually causation. Where the protected disclosure has more than a trivial influence on the detrimental treatment of the partner, causation will be established."

(c) Time limits

The primary limitation period for discrimination and whistleblowing claims is three months from the act complained of.

It is mandatory to go through the Advisory, Conciliation and Arbitration Service early conciliation process before commencing an employment tribunal claim, which can extend the time limit by a short period.

The strict time limit is likely to focus minds on the potential for settlement. If constructive discussion does not materialise, a partner may have little option but to issue claims protectively with the danger that positions become entrenched.

5.3 Documentation

Gathering evidence is likely to be key to a successful challenge to a partner's involuntary retirement. In addition to express rights and the default regimes, partners can make use of their data subject access request rights.

Information requests generally can prove tactically useful for a partner. Responses to data subject access requests are resource hungry and may uncover helpful material. Requests for books or records pursuant to the default regime or terms of the partnership deed may be ventilated in arbitration or the courts and lead to the recovery of costs. A request for documents may include the following:

- communications in relation to any proposal for involuntary retirement or other detrimental action;
- information considered by the management committee involved in the proposal;
- communications between partners relating to a vote regarding proposed voluntary retirement; and
- minutes on the subject of any vote and proposed/final resolutions.

Legal advice concerning the firm's intention to involuntarily retire a partner paid for by the firm is likely to be a 'book' or 'record'. Absent any restrictive provisions limiting information available to partners, the partner will have the right to see this advice. Advice is usually taken by certain members directly in order to avoid this risk. Privilege will attach to confidential communications between the firm or its lawyers and third parties or other documents created by the firm or its lawyers which come into existence once litigation is in contemplation and which are for the dominant purpose of use in litigation.

6. Business protection by the firm – risks for the partner

A retiring partner may not intend to stop working. Indeed, many retiring partners have plans to start a new business, move to another business in a different role or consult for a host of professional practices on issues such as strategic planning and business advice. The firm will often be cautious to protect itself from unlawful competition.

Enforcing restrictive covenants is the usual method. Partners should also remain vigilant as to their express and implied duties while they remain a partner, including during any period of notice. The High Court has ordered forfeiture of a portion of profit share following breach of contractual and fiduciary duties of an LLP member preparing to compete. In that particular case, under the terms of the LLP agreement, the portion forfeited was held to be a reward for undertaking fiduciary duties/remuneration and not a reward for the partner's ownership interest. This will require a careful consideration of the facts of each case.

Post-termination restrictions are often aimed at preventing partners from:

- moving to a competitor for a specified period following retirement;
- encouraging other partners and staff to leave or offering

employment or partnership to those colleagues at their new firm;
- soliciting or dealing with clients or trade connections for a specified period; and
- interfering with the firm's business in any other respect.

Restrictive covenants must go no further than is reasonably necessary to protect legitimate business interests. These include the partnership's goodwill, its confidential information, the stability of its workforce and its client connections.

In general, partner-restrictive covenants are more likely to be enforceable than employee restrictions. In a traditional partnership context, *Bridge v Deacons* remains good law. Thirty-five years ago, the Judicial Committee of the Privy Council held that a covenant preventing an ex-partner from acting as a solicitor for a period of five years for any party that had been a client of the firm at the time of his departure or in the preceding three years was enforceable.

The position between a LLP and an ex-member is less clear. However, the prevailing view is that members of LLPs will be treated by the courts more like traditional partners than like employees – largely

"Restrictive covenants must go no further than is reasonably necessary to protect legitimate business interests. These include the partnership's goodwill, its confidential information, the stability of its workforce and its client connections."

because a member has an interest in a share of the profits of the firm and an interest in the preservation of goodwill.

Until recently, most partnership lawyers questioned whether *Bridge v Deacons* would be decided differently today. However, it was recently applied in a case providing support to the proposition that onerous and lengthy covenants may be enforced against members of an LLP.

The courts interpret the natural meaning of a restrictive covenant and judge reasonableness (taking account the firm's legitimate business interest) at the time it was drafted. Where a covenant refers to competition, the starting point is whether there is competition between the firm and prospective firm. The courts will consider the duration of the restriction, its geographical scope and what it prevents the departing partner from doing – in particular, whether the restraint exceeds the scope of the relevant business and client base.

Increasingly, firms are including anti-team move provisions in LLP agreements as a means of attempting to prevent members from leaving together to join a competitor. These clauses have not been fully tested in the courts. The prevailing view among practitioners is that they are likely to be difficult to enforce.

'Waiting room' clauses are also likely to be subject to scrutiny as restraints of trade.

If a post-termination restrictive covenant is held unreasonable, it is void and unenforceable.

If the partner concludes that a clause is likely to be unenforceable because of the way it is drafted, he or she should also consider whether the covenant could nonetheless be rendered enforceable by using a 'blue pencil' to remove the objectionable words in the covenant.

Where a restrictive covenant is considered enforceable and has been breached, the firm generally initially has two options. It can issue High Court proceedings and apply for an interim injunction to restrain the breach pending trial. Springboard injunctions may also be available to cancel an unfair advantage in certain circumstances, typically involving misuse of confidential information. Alternatively, a firm may sue the partner for damages. How the retiring partner responds to such a claim (usually ventilated in pre-action correspondence) will depend on the circumstances of the case and the covenants. Disputes may be resolved by way of contractual undertakings given to the firm. This may avoid the costs of proceedings and the risks of having to give undertakings to the court, fortified by a penal notice. Breach of a penal notice may result in a party being held in contempt of court.

> *"Demonstrating a commitment to finding a way through conflict may resonate with the firm and pave the way to a constructive discussion about settlement."*

7. The deal and beyond

"A little consideration, a little thought for others, makes all the difference" – Eeyore (*Winnie the Pooh*)

At some point, demonstrating a commitment to finding a way through conflict may resonate with the firm and pave the way to a constructive discussion about settlement.

Considerations may include the following:

- Retirement date: There may be scope for negotiation around garden leave or payments in lieu of notice if remaining in role is important for future plans. If there is to be a period of garden leave, is it appropriate to vary any agreement to accommodate any relaxed restrictions?
- Financial entitlements: Often, agreements will prescribe that payments will be made in the same manner as if the retiring partner continued to be a partner. Will the firm make a special distribution of the partner's current account and payments in relation to any open financial year with a balancing payment following closing of accounts in due course? Can repayment of capital be expedited or the firm step into the partner's shoes? Enhanced entitlements connected with voluntary retirement –

for example, the effect of notice requirements or the fact the partner would otherwise be eligible for soft landing benefits – may be useful in articulating a minimum expectation in the absence of wrongdoing. They may facilitate discussion around retention of profit share for longer, particularly if the mechanics of expulsion or compulsory retirement are onerous or if voting requirements may not be met.

- Waiver of claims: Is this reciprocal? Effective waiver of employment rights requires the partner to seek advice from a lawyer, who will need to sign a certificate confirming that he or she has advised the departing partner of the terms and effect of the retirement deed and the impact of signing the deed on the partner's ability to bring any claims in the employment tribunal.
- Restrictions: Is there scope for these to be relaxed or removed?
- Confidentiality clauses: Partners should ensure that there are appropriate carve-outs to support future plans. Typical associated provisions would include a reciprocal 'non-derogatory comment' clause.
- Announcements and references: Appropriate messaging and references can assume great significance in negotiations.
- Ongoing membership of benefits schemes (if permitted by the scheme), or retention of firm property such as a vehicle, mobile phone (or transfer of number) and laptop.
- Payment of legal fees in connection with the exit and for tax advice for an agreed period.
- Outplacement support.
- Arrangements for forwarding private telephone messages, emails and post. An automatic reply may be agreed for email communications.
- Access to documents.
- Retention of know-how and precedents.
- Provision for the partner's estate to benefit from any payments due if his or her death precedes payments.
- Consultancy: If the partner will continue as a consultant to the firm, a separate agreement is advisable to manage the new relationship between the parties.

A useful guiding principle for a partner is to focus on priorities and be prepared to give on things that cost him or her nothing, but are likely to be important to the firm.

III. Accounting and practical considerations

Paul Beber
Cecil Associates

1. Introduction

It is testimony to its enduring attraction that, despite the move in recent years towards more corporate-based structures, partnership status – particularly for aspiring younger professionals – is still highly sought after. For all professional persons, whether at the beginning or end of their working lives, one of the great advantages of partnership – and perhaps the reason for its continued attraction – is its flexibility. Unlike, for example, in limited companies, a partner can wake up one morning and decide that he or she no longer wishes to continue practising as a lawyer, an accountant or whatever other profession he or she is in. Then, with relatively minimal fuss, he or she can retire.

Of course, it should not happen just like that; planning should take place for retirement well in advance. It should be a given that all professional practices have a partnership agreement, agreed upon at the time of entrance into partnership and updated from time to time by agreement and as required by circumstances, as well as by professional and legislative changes. These agreements should include full and proper governance provisions covering retirement.

It is not, however, just a question of the partnership agreement setting out procedures for partners retiring, when they should retire, notice periods, the basis of final accounting for their shares of profits and how they will be paid out. There are also issues such as succession and management to consider – and most important of all, the lifeblood of professional practices: client service.

This chapter focuses on the financial and practical aspects of retirement, but consideration of other aspects should not be overlooked. Finance and accounting issues can play a major part in the transition from working life to retirement, for both the continuing partnership and the retiree. Consideration of these can set the tone and make transition either more or less difficult.

An important point for the retiree to remember is that, while an insider and a partner, the principle of *uberrimae fidei* between partners is (or should be) a given; once on the outside, however, different rules potentially apply. The 'field' is far more open and the responsibility of finance staff and advisers is to the ongoing business, not the retiree.

Although most professional practices are now structured as LLPs, there are still a considerable number of unincorporated partnerships governed by the Partnership Act 1890. As partners in these practices have unlimited liability to creditors, care around issues concerning liabilities requires even greater attention than for LLPs.

"While an insider and a partner, the principle of uberrimae fidei *between partners is (or should be) a given; once on the outside, however, different rules potentially apply."*

This chapter focuses on the retirement of full equity partners. However, many of the issues discussed apply equally to fixed share and/or salaried partners.

2. Retirement date

Historically, for reasons of taxation advantage, the favoured year-end for professional practices was 30 April (or 31 May or 30 June). Changes some years ago to the taxation system for self-employed persons such as partners in professional partnerships have led to an increasing number adopting 31 March year-ends, which simplifies the calculation of taxation payable for retirees; 31 December as the calendar year-end is also increasingly popular.

Usually, a partner shares profits only until the date of retirement; consequently, the date of retirement is highly important to the retirement process. Critically, to determine the profit share due to the retiree, accounts must normally be drawn up to the retirement date. Consequently, and whatever the year-end, the most convenient date for retirement for accounting purposes is the financial year-end of the practice. This enables the annual accounts of the practice to serve also as accounts for retirement purposes.

It is not unusual, therefore, for partnership agreements to specify that this is the only date for retirement by due notice. Unfortunately, death, ill health and unforeseen circumstances are no respecters of financial year-ends. In such circumstances, partnership agreements often include provisions such as basing profit shares for the year of retirement on average previous profit shares.

This is certainly the case where the retirement date is towards the beginning of the financial year. Where the business is seasonal biased to near the year-end date and there is a retirement towards the end of the financial year, shares of profits may instead be based on a *pro rata* share of actual profits for the year.

3. Impact of partnership structure and profit-sharing arrangements

Modern partnerships have tended to develop increasingly complex legal structures, driven not only by taxation, but also by client needs and diversification where incentivisation of non-professional qualified staff is important.

Most commonly, alongside the professional partnership, many practices have a limited company that employs all staff and provides their services and facilities to the practice (ie, a service company). Driven predominantly by taxation – the cost of working capital being significantly lower for corporates compared to partnerships – an equity partner's capital account can often predominantly be represented not by capital that he or she has left in the partnership itself, but rather by his or her share of the shareholders' funds of the service company.

Corporate structures also exist alongside professional partnerships, providing specific client services. Accountancy partnerships, for example, have historically maintained management consultancy practices; and since the Legal Services Act 2007, law firms have increasingly looked to adopt alternative business structures for part, if not all, of their business.

In such circumstances, where there are corporate entities alongside the partnership itself, partner retirement must address both partnership and corporate requirements, usually at or around the same time.

Partnership profit-sharing arrangements, where profit sharing is based on partner personal performance, must also take into account partner retirement, especially where the retirement date is known or agreed well in advance. New business generation and chargeable time can be adversely affected by impending retirement; existing clients and contacts can be less certain to refer business and the partnership should be looking to the retiree to transition clients and contacts. Performance-based profit sharing, particularly in the last year of partnership, must take these factors into account.

4. Accounts at the date of retirement

4.1 General

Given that an equity partner is entitled to a share of profits of the partnership until the date of retirement, accounts to that date are a fundamental requirement. The partnership agreement should include provisions as how these accounts are prepared and the retirement arrangements should also encompass any special arrangements that may be required.

LLPs are required by law to prepare annual accounts that show a true and fair view. Although no such law exists for 1890 partnerships, accounts complying with UK Generally Accepted Accounting Principles, or alternatively International Accounting Standards, are required for all partnerships to be prepared for taxation purposes by Her Majesty's Revenue & Customs. For most professional partnerships, this means that the annual accounts will be drawn up with accounting policies in accordance with FRS102; larger ones may adopt FRS101 or IAS.

"Where the partnership is required for the annual accounts to adopt a change of accounting policy, careful thought will need to be given to the impact for the purposes of retirement."

Whatever the accounting standards adopted by the partnership, from a retiree's point of view, the impact of such standards needs careful consideration. It is normal that accounts must be prepared on a consistent basis, using consistent policies and accounting bases. However, where the partnership is required for the annual accounts to adopt a change of accounting policy, careful thought will need to be given to the impact for the purposes of retirement. The retiree may need to insist that adverse impacts of changes in policy are removed for the purposes of calculating his or her share of profits for the year of retirement.

The annual accounts measure assets and liabilities, and by result profits available to share between partners, as of a specific date. Estimates and judgement are an integral part of drawing up such accounts. However, longer term, the estimates and judgements at a particular time are superseded by actual known amounts. The retiree is advised to consider provision in the retirement arrangements for look-back adjustments.

4.2 Valuation of assets

Freehold and leasehold property: It is unusual for professional practices to own freehold or long leasehold property; the norm is that such property is held in a separate partnership. However, where the partnership owns the property, it will be included in the accounts at either historic cost or valuation, which itself may not be up to date. On a partner retirement, it is usually essential that the property is revalued professionally.

Art and antique collections: It is increasingly fashionable in many partnerships for offices to be decorated with art and antiques. As with property, consideration will need to be given to valuing such assets.

Equipment, furniture and fittings: Equipment, furniture and fittings acquired by the practice will normally be depreciated (expensed) over the expected lives of the various classes of assets. Computer equipment is often depreciated over three years given the pace of change and therefore obsolescence; whereas furniture and fittings will usually last five, seven or even 10 years.

Consideration needs to be given annually to the useful lives of such fixed assets; but in practice, too often previous methods are just followed. Both the firm and the retiree should consider whether the depreciation policies (and any residual values) have been properly considered.

Trade debtors: Trade debtors usually consist of bills rendered to clients and disbursements laid out on their behalf not yet billed to them. At each year-end, every practice will consider whether such debtors are recoverable and, to the extent that they are judged to be irrecoverable, provision for bad and doubtful debts will be made. Given that many professional practices have unpaid debtors' balances well over six months old, such provisions are often very material.

Ultimately, whether a debtor balance is good or bad is an actual fact. If the debtor does not pay eventually, it is definitely bad. If it does pay, then any provision made has been recovered. For the retiree, it is sensible to require a look-back review and additional post-retirement payment if debtors provided against are subsequently recovered – certainly where the debtor amount provided against is a significant amount.

Accrued income/work-in-progress: Accrued income has for many years been required under standard accounting policies, to be valued at selling price, not as previously for work-in-progress at the lower of cost and net realisable value. For annual accounts, accrued income is valued using estimates of whether overall the time is recoverable and recovery rates for time incurred over the period ending on the accounts date.

As with provisions made against trade debtors for recoverability, it is sensible for the retiree to require a look-back review and possibly adjustments where write-downs of time incurred are significant and the impact of estimates may be material, if incorrect.

Contingent fees: Under standard accounting policies, fees that are contingent at the year-end date are not brought into account. Such fees can be extremely significant in certain circumstances and for certain types of professional practice (eg, personal injury claims firms). It is not unusual for such income not to be estimated as at the date of retirement; instead, the retiree and the partnership need, in the absence of a pre-existing alternative, to agree a method under which contingent fees are accounted for subsequently and the retiree's due proportion paid as a post-retirement payment.

Personal equipment: An area of difficulty can be items of personal equipment – most frequently cars, which are owned or leased by the partnership for the benefit of the retiring partners. On retirement, the retiree will usually be required to buy out the equipment at the then value or, in the case of leased assets, to take over the leasing cost.

Other assets: One of the problems in looking at accounts is recognising not only what is there, but also – just as importantly – what is not there. If an asset is written off, it no longer appears in the

"Liabilities – debts owed by the partnership – will usually be fully accounted for by the partnership and when a partner is retiring, the accounts department is usually vigilant to ensure that provision is made for all liabilities."

"Stamp duty land tax on leases can be a significant figure and is a cost that can be argued should be expensed over the period of the lease, but it may well be written off as part of premises costs or legal and professional expenditure; the effect is to depress the amount of all partners' capital accounts, including the retiree."

balance sheet and the size of amounts disclosed as expenses in the profit and loss account does not facilitate easy detection of assets that have been expensed.

For example, stamp duty land tax on leases can be a significant figure and is a cost that can be argued should be expensed over the period of the lease, but it may well be written off as part of premises costs or legal and professional expenditure; the effect is to depress the amount of all partners' capital accounts, including the retiree.

Other assets that may well be written off include computer software, whether developed in-house or externally. The cost incurred in any year may well have benefits in succeeding years, but if written off immediately as an expense, such benefit is not shared with the retiree.

The retiree needs to review the accounts in detail – not just for the final period of partnership, but also for prior periods.

4.3 Liabilities

General liabilities: Liabilities – debts owed by the partnership – will usually be fully accounted for by the partnership and when a partner is retiring, the accounts department is usually vigilant to ensure that provision is made for all liabilities. The amount of some liabilities, however, may not be totally quantifiable as at the accounts date and therefore estimates may be required by the management of the partnership. The retiree should ensure that he or she is aware of what estimates have been made and that such are reasonable.

If the partnership uses FRS101 for its accounts, care is required in assessing the impact of lease liabilities compared to the carrying value of short leasehold premises.

Provisions: Estimates are most frequently used and can be very subjective, where provisions must be made for certain liabilities. In this regard, a key area is that of claims asserted against the partnership for negligence and similar. Other major areas include restructuring provisions and leasehold premises dilapidations.

Claims against the partnership are usually covered by professional indemnity insurance. However, in the event of a successful claim, the partnership must pay the excess; and additionally, if the claim is more than the level of insurance cover, the amount of the claim over the level of applicable insurance. Such liabilities will have to be estimated at the accounts date.

Restructuring provisions – for example, in relation to the closure of an office and/or redundancies – are usually provided for in accounts when the decision is made by management to carry out the restructuring. The usual reason behind such decisions is that this improves long-term efficiency and profitability. From the retiree's point of view, he or she has borne his or her share of the excess costs historically, and unless the impact on him or her personally of the restructuring provision is adjusted for (ie, removed), he or she will also bear the cost of the changes, but not have a share of the longer-term cost savings.

Strictly speaking, dilapidations should be provided by the partnership over the period of the lease. However, estimates of the cost can vary very widely. Additionally, the landlord's intentions for the premises after the partnership leaves can significantly influence any claim for dilapidations.

The retiree should carefully review all provisions made by the partnership, to ensure that they have been made reasonably. However, given that the amounts of provisions are often very subjective, retirement agreements should include look-back reviews and, for restructuring and similar amounts, adjustment to remove the impact on the retiree. Under look-back reviews, provisions made are re-examined post the retirement accounts date – usually on an annual basis at minimum and for a number of years. Any excess provisions are then accounted for proportionately to the retiree as a post-retirement payment.

Contingent liabilities: Unlike provisions, contingent liabilities are not provided for in the accounts of the partnership, but are noted as potential liabilities. Examples could include guarantees given to third parties which could potentially fall back on the partnership, which must then meet an expense.

As no provision has been made in the accounts, the retiree will not have borne his or her share of such liabilities. The partnership may well require some form of post-retirement contribution if the liability crystallises. This is always a difficult area and one where the retiree's desire to have closure may require some form of negotiation as to the extent of any liability to be shared.

Audit/external review: The accounts of the partnership should be prepared by the partnership itself on a good-faith basis for all partners. As the retiree is a partner as at the accounts date (he or she retires with effect from the accounts date – that is, 1 May for 30 April retirement, and the accounts would be to 30 April close of business/midnight); this should include the retiree as well. However, the retiree is advised to be cautious, given that he or she will no longer be a partner when the accounts are actually prepared.

"An audit cannot be relied upon by the individual retiree. The duties of the auditors auditing an LLP are normally only to the LLP itself and not individual members, whether continuing or retiring."

Nevertheless, the retiree may be asked to approve the accounts, which will be the retirement date accounts.

The annual accounts of LLPs must be audited formally by external accountants if the partnership is not regarded for statutory purposes as a small entity. Smaller partnerships (by statutory definition) and 1890 partnerships do not require an audit.

Although an audit may give the retiree some comfort that the accounts have been externally reviewed, an audit cannot be relied upon by the individual retiree. The duties of the auditors auditing an LLP are normally only to the LLP itself and not individual members, whether continuing or retiring. Furthermore, an audit is carried out only to discover material errors; what is not material to the partnership as a whole may well be material or at least very significant to an individual partner, particularly a retiree.

Given the degree of subjectivity that is applied in many areas of the accounts and the limitations of external audits, the retiree should carefully consider carrying out his or her own review of the accounts of the partnership or employing specialists to conduct such a review. While this review may concentrate on the accounts at the date of retirement, some form of review of prior year accounts may also be required.

"With the growth in size of partnerships and the creation of seemingly ever-larger firms, payments for goodwill on accession to equity partnership and receipt of goodwill on retirement have become the exception rather than the rule."

5. Goodwill and anti-embarrassment arrangements

The partnership asset that most frequently is not included in its balance sheet is goodwill. Even if the partnership has acquired another practice and actually paid some goodwill, it is usually written off over a period of years and then disappears from the balance sheet along with any reckoning for a partner retiring – despite him or her bearing a portion of the cost.

With the growth in size of partnerships and the creation of seemingly ever-larger firms, payments for goodwill on accession to equity partnership and receipt of goodwill on retirement have become the exception rather than the rule. In most partnerships, new equity partners now expect to come in with nothing and leave with nothing; the injection of a capital contribution is an amount owed to them and returned when they leave – it is not a payment for goodwill whose value changes.

Yet partners work all their professional lives to build up a client and contact base; they may initially be given some of this by other partners, but they must then develop this to help the partnership business grow. They are then expected to give this up to the next generation for nothing! Compare this to an entrepreneur who builds up a business and then sells it. If the sale proceeds are more than the net tangible assets, the entrepreneur will receive in effect payment for goodwill – the ability to earn profits.

An exception to the general rule is small accountancy practices. Accountancy partnerships benefit from the advantage of having recurring clients (the transactional nature of legal work being one of the arguments against paying for goodwill in legal practices), and it is not unusual for owner partners of smaller accountancy practices to sell their business and receive a goodwill payment based on gross recurring fees (GRF). Payment may be over a period of time and depend on the acquirer being able to maintain GRF; but still, it is payment for goodwill.

In the early 2000s, accountancy practices started floating on the UK stock markets, raising capital from investors and acting as consolidators, acquiring other accountancy and related activity practices. These entities paid goodwill to acquire medium-sized as well as smaller practices.

Most of these enterprises ended in failure, but the Legal Services Act 2007 introduced the concept of the practice of law by multi-disciplinary practices and has thereby facilitated external equity fundraising. Take-up of such external funding has been relatively slow – probably due to the recession that started in 2008 – but it does appear to be gradually growing and there are now publicly listed (quoted) legal practice companies.

The concept, therefore, of retiring partners receiving payment for goodwill is not one that should be dismissed. One of the biggest problems facing professional partnerships is that of succession; retirees may well be more incentivised to act for the longer-term benefit of the partnership if they are paid goodwill on retirement. Also, payment for goodwill can act as a safeguard for the continuing practice; if payment is made, it is not unreasonable to obtain a non-compete arrangement with the retiree covering clients, employees and the business.

In the absence of payments for goodwill, retirees may well seek to try to take their clients with them and continue servicing such clients. Where payment is made for goodwill and non-compete agreements, the courts are more likely to enforce post-termination restrictions.

Given that goodwill is a capital payment and must be paid out of net of tax income, an alternative which is more tax efficient for the partnership is some form of annuity, payable for a set number of years. As the retiree does not have to continue to work to receive the annuity, it is in effect payment for goodwill.

Whatever the rights and wrongs of the goodwill payment argument, if the retiree is to leave without payment and hand over his or her clients and contacts, at the very least he or she should seek to negotiate some form of anti-embarrassment arrangement. Goodwill relies upon the next owner to continue to be valuable; but if the successors can realise a value for goodwill after the retiree leaves, it is only fair that such benefit is shared with the retiree.

Anti-embarrassment arrangements apportion a share of any goodwill consideration received by the partnership to be paid to the retiree. Typically, the share paid out will decrease over time; it may be, say, 90% to 100% if the sale occurs within a year, declining to nil over up to five years.

6. Non-partnership assets

Freehold/long leasehold property: Non-partnership assets that are affected by a partner retirement are usually office premises, owned by the retiree either in part or wholly and let to the partnership. Given that professional partnerships are generally regarded as excellent tenants, such investments are quite attractive for partners with available capital.

"The actual profit for the last year of equity partnership may take some time to calculate, then be reviewed and agreed by everybody concerned. However, bar unforeseen matters arising, reasonable estimates should have been made well before the day of the amount payable to the retiree."

The partnership can benefit from the close relationship with its landlord, especially if it encounters financial difficulties. However, as a general rule, if the premises occupied by the partnership is owned by one or more of the partners, to avoid future problems, all transactions and arrangements should be on an arm's-length basis.

This applies especially post-retirement. Both the retiree and the partnership should review the lease arrangements as part of the retirement agenda and ensure that they are adequate.

Investments: The other most common non-partnership assets are other investments – usually into companies or businesses outside the partnership – which have been made available to some or all equity partners. There should be some form of investment or shareholder agreement entered into at the time the investment is made and, if required, also an agreement between the investor partners involved.

The investment made by the retiree will likely continue post-retirement. If the investor partners have acted in concert previously, they may well need to continue to do so. The relationship between the investor partners should be properly agreed at the time of retirement, if not already in place. This should include provision for sharing information received with the retiree, as well as ensuring that he or she is consulted before any 'joint' decision is made.

7. Financial settlement/payments

The last day arrives. The farewell party is held. The retiree shakes everybody's hands and leaves. The partnership has known that this day is coming and should have a financial plan that includes making provision for the amounts payable to the retiree. Leaving aside any payment for goodwill, the retiree will be due his or her partnership capital and undrawn share of profits.

The actual profit for the last year of equity partnership may take some time to calculate, then be reviewed and agreed by everybody concerned. However, bar unforeseen matters arising, reasonable estimates should have been made well before the day of the amount payable to the retiree.

Many professional practices avoid being financed by bank loans and overdrafts, with the result that partners' capital and current accounts may well be very substantial. In these circumstances, and assuming that retirement is planned in advance, it is sensible in the last few years leading up to a partner retiring for capital to start to be repaid to the retiree well before the retirement date.

Whether this is possible or not, the remaining amount due to the retiree (absent any express agreement otherwise) is a liability of the partnership (for an LLP) or the personal liability of continuing partners (for an 1890 partnership). The payment period of this liability will depend on the future cash flow of the practice (ie, its ability to pay), but it must also take into account the cash requirements of the retiree.

Many partnerships have continued to finance themselves by retaining the tax due on partnership profits. This is notwithstanding that, for many years, tax payable by partners on their share of profits is no longer a joint liability, but individual. From the day of retirement, the retiree will need to have the cash to pay outstanding tax as it falls due. The timing of payments to them therefore must take such personal liabilities into account.

As already noted, once the retiree ceases to be a partner – or member if the structure is a LLP – the capital and other amounts owed to them are liabilities of the business. In effect, the retiree is lending money to the partnership. As such, two other key factors when loan moneys are involved must be considered: interest and security.

In respect of interest, it is essential from the retiree's standpoint that moneys due to the retiree are not treated as cheap forms of funding. For this reason, and to encourage repayment, the rate of interest is normally equivalent to that paid by the partnership to its bankers for overdrafts or loans.

Security is more problematic. If the LLP has given security over its assets to its bankers, second charges can be impracticable. Additionally, it may indicate some sense of distrust for former partners to require security.

The usual period for repayment of capital and current accounts, and any other payments due to the retiree, is two to three years. If the partnership is seeking a longer period than this or if its finances are not in good shape, it is even more important for the retiree to consider security, or possibly discounting the total amount receivable for quicker repayment.

The amounts repayable to the retiree will need to include the value of shares where the partnership structure includes corporate entities. The share of value for service companies is usually based on net asset value; for other entities, it depends on the shareholder agreement between the partners. The method under which the retiree is paid out can be by way of the continuing partners buying out the retiree, the companies involved buying back their shares or, if the company is no longer required, winding it up through a members' voluntary liquidation.

"The retiree should seek undertakings from the continuing partnership that he or she maintain professional indemnity insurance, at least at the same level as historically, for a period of no less than six years post-retirement."

Whatever the method of realisation of value, the amount owed is normally added to the total payable to the retiree and the agreed repayment schedule. There are potential different taxation implications for the retiree, depending on the method of realisation.

8. Post-retirement issues

Post-retirement, the partnership may still need to call upon the retiree for assistance. Aside from possible post-retirement consultancy, the retiree may need to assist in dealing with any claims made against the partnership in respect of work undertaken by the retiree.

The partnership should have cover from professional indemnity insurance; even so, there are reputational issues and therefore partnership agreements usually include a requirement for retirees to give their time freely to assist, with only direct out-of-pocket expenses being covered by the partnership.

Unless already provided for, the retiree should seek undertakings from the continuing partnership that he or she maintain professional indemnity insurance, at least at the same level as historically, for a period of no less than six years post-retirement. Professional indemnity insurance deals with claims on an arising basis: a claim may be made for work done several years previously; but from the insurer's standpoint, cover is the insurance at the date of the claim, not when the work was carried out.

The retiree should also consider, if not already in the partnership agreement, seeking indemnities from the continuing partners for future liabilities, especially in the case of an 1890 partnership with unlimited liability. Even with LLPs, personal guarantees may have been given, for example, to the partnership bankers or landlords; the indemnity should last until the personal guarantees have been released.

Finally, while an equity partner, the retiree may well have received a range of benefits, including medical insurance, permanent health and life insurance, as well as a range of other 'employment-type' benefits. These may no longer be available to the retiree. The retiree will need to consider alternatives before retirement, if such benefits are still required afterwards. For medical benefits, for example, some insurers may allow group schemes to include former partners or facilitate their transfer into a bespoke group.

IV. Tax considerations

Nicky Owen
Crowe U.K. LLP

1. Introduction
You are thinking of retiring as a partner. It may be that you have been a self-employed partner for many years and are unsure of the tax implications of retiring and when tax payments will fall due. In the past, your firm may have dealt with your tax payments on your behalf and this may not have been on your radar; post-retirement, that will change and you will be responsible for calculating and arranging settlement of your tax liabilities.

2. Lead-up to retirement
It is a good idea to have a plan in place that enables you to pass your practice over to your successors. That plan will look different for each partner and may include stepping down the equity ladder, changing working hours or becoming a fixed-share partner, a salaried partner or a consultant. Such changes will affect your tax position. You will need to agree your plans with the firm and include timelines so that the new arrangements work for you, the firm and clients.

3. Equity changes
As an equity partner, you might have been involved in the firm's decision making in some way. Stepping down from equity means stepping away from that involvement. Stepping away from equity should mean less risk and a change in the level of capital you have invested in the business.

Changing your equity status within an LLP may trigger a review of the salaried members' legislation in respect of your status and, assuming that you continue to fail one of the three tests, you will continue to be treated as self-employed for tax purposes. If, however, you pass all of the tests, you should be treated as employed and the firm will need to deduct pay as you earn (PAYE) and pay employers' National Insurance contributions (NICs).

Salaried members' legislation is a chapter on its own; however, it involves tests that look at:

- your level of profits;
- the element of profits linked to the performance of the business as a whole;
- your level of capital; and
- the influence you have on the firm.

An experienced finance partner at the firm or the firm's advisers should be fully aware of the implications and accustomed to regular reviews to ensure that partners do not fall foul of this legislation.

4. Profit share

Changing your equity status, becoming a fixed share partner or reducing your hours will all impact on your profit share. Your tax position will also be affected: reducing your profit share will correspondingly reduce your income tax and NICs payable. For those paying tax and NICs totalling 47%, for every reduction in profit share of £10,000, their net income will reduce by £5,300.

Consider whether you will need to supplement your income from other sources to accommodate this change in your life.

5. Capital invested in the firm

In previous years, it is likely that you will have paid capital into the firm; now that you are retiring, the capital will be repaid in due course. There are tax implications that need to be considered:

- Will changing your equity status reduce your level of capital within the firm? If so, when will capital be repaid – in full or by regular payments over time? Your level of capital invested into the firm is linked to one of the salaried members' legislation tests and care must thus be taken to ensure that the repayment of capital while you are still a partner does not change your self-employed status. When capital is repaid by a firm, Her Majesty's Revenue & Customs (HMRC) deems that the capital repaid is in respect of capital that has been loaned in the first instance. Therefore, if capital has been borrowed and the capital repaid has not been used to repay the loan, the interest relief is restricted. From the date of retirement, no tax relief is available on loan interest paid on loans to acquire capital.

- How will you fund any loan interest payable after retirement?
- Will the firm pay interest to you on capital still held by the firm after your retirement? If so, you will pay tax on the interest paid by the firm.
- What rate of interest will the firm pay?
- How will you invest your capital repayment?
- Is it tax efficient to use it to pay off any partnership capital loans or other loans?

6. Salaried member/partner

If, as part of the process of stepping down within the firm, you become salaried, then your employment status will change from self-employed to employed. The difference is substantial.

Being treated as employed means that your profits are taxable under PAYE and tax is deducted from your drawings each month and paid over to HMRC. You will be subject to Class 1 NICs on your share of profits. The firm will pay employers' NICs on your share of profits.

You will complete employee pages on your tax return and not partner pages.

"If capital has been borrowed and the capital repaid has not been used to repay the loan, the interest relief is restricted."

7. Retiring as a partner

When retiring as a partner, in your final tax year as a partner you will be taxed on the profits from the end of the previous accounting period ending in the previous tax year to the date of retirement from the firm.

The tax implications will depend on the date you retire and the accounting date of the firm.

Detailed below are a few examples showing the basis period on which you will be taxed in the tax years concerned.

7.1 Firm has 31 March accounting year-end

(a) You retire at the year-end date

You will be taxed on your taxable profit share to the date of the accounting year-end. There will be no taxable profit share in the tax year following; you are not a partner of the firm.

Example 1: You are retiring on 31 March 2020

Tax year	Basis period
2018/19	Year ended 31 March 2019
2019/20	Year ended 31 March 2020
2020/21	No partnership income

(b) You retire part-way through the accounting year

You will be taxed on your taxable profit share to the date of your retirement. There will be no taxable profit share after the date of your retirement, and this will affect the tax year in which you retire and future tax years when you are not a partner of the firm.

Example 2: You are retiring on 30 September 2020

Tax year	Basis period
2018/19	Year ended 31 March 2019
2019/20	Year ended 31 March 2020
2020/21	6 months to 30 September 2020
2021/22	No partnership income

7.2 Firm's accounting year-end is not coterminous with tax year

If the firm has an accounting year-end that is not coterminous with the tax year, you will need to take into account your overlap profits brought forward. Partners tend to struggle with the concept that they may have worked for only a few months within the tax year, but are being taxed on a whole year's taxable profit less overlap relief, which – by reason of inflation, changes in profit share and the success of the business – may have limited impact on their net taxable profit share in the year of retirement.

"When retiring as a partner, in your final tax year as a partner you will be taxed on the profits from the end of the previous accounting period ending in the previous tax year to the date of retirement from the firm."

Usually, overlap profits are generated when you first become a partner in a firm that does not have an accounting year-end date that is coterminous with the tax year-end of 5 April. HMRC treats all year-ends from 31 March to 5 April as coterminous.

Overlap profits are all part of the process of becoming taxable on the accounting year ending in the tax year. To achieve this, there needs to be some adjustment when you first become a partner and when you retire.

For example, when you initially became a partner, in the first year of assessment as a partner, you would have been taxed on your partnership profit share from the date you became a partner to the end of the tax year. In the second year of assessment, you would have been taxed on your partnership income for the first 12 months. Hence, there will be a period of profits on which you have been taxed twice. On your tax return, these are disclosed as overlap profits and are shown on your return each year as a memo, until they are utilised when you leave. Overlap profits can also be generated or changed if the firm changes its accounting year-end date.

(a) You retire at the accounting year-end date

You will be taxed on your taxable profit share to the date of the accounting year-end, less overlap relief brought forward. There will be no taxable profit share post the retirement date.

Example 3: The firm has an accounting date of 30 April and you are retiring on 30 April 2020

Tax year	Basis period
2018/19	Year ended 30 April 2018
2019/20	Year ended 30 April 2019
2020/21	Year ended 30 April 2020
	Less overlap profits brought forward
2021/22	No partnership income

Put some numbers into the equation and assume the following:

- Taxable profits to 30 April 2020 are £360,000.
- Overlap profits brought forward are £55,000.

What partnership profits will you be taxed on in the tax year 2020/21?

	£
Taxable profits to 30 April 2020	360,000
Less overlap profits brought forward	(55,000)
Assessable partnership profits	£305,000

It is not unusual for partners to expect to be taxed on one month's profit share; but this is not what happens.

(b) You retire part-way through the accounting year

You will be taxed on your taxable profit share from the end of the previous accounting period ending in the previous tax year to the date of retirement, less overlap profits brought forward. There will be no taxable profit share after the date of your retirement and this will affect the tax year in which you retire and future tax years; you are not a partner of the firm.

Example 4: The firm has an accounting date of 30 April and you are bringing forward your retirement date by one month to 31 March 2020

Tax year	Basis period
2018/19	Year ended 30 April 2018
2019/20	Year ended 30 April 2019
	11 months to 31 March 2020
	Less overlap profits brought forward
2020/21	No partnership income

Put some numbers into the equation and assume the following:

- Taxable profits to 30 April 2019 are £340,000.
- Taxable profits for the 11 months to 31 March 2020 are £330,000.
- Overlap profits brought forward are £55,000.

What partnership profits will you be taxed on in the tax year 2019/20?

	£
Taxable profits to 30 April 2019	340,000
Taxable profits for the 11 months to 31 March 2020	330,000
Less overlap profits brought forward	(55,000)
Assessable partnership profits	£615,000

By bringing forward the retirement date, an additional £275,000 will potentially be taxed at 45% in the tax year 2019/20 by reference to your top marginal rate for that tax year. By contrast, if the retirement date had been delayed, £150,000 would have suffered tax at lower rates, by making use of the 20% and 40% income tax bands in the tax year 2020/21. You will have brought forward the date when tax is payable; you must also consider the impact of NICs, which have a 9% band before dropping down to 2%.

8. Retirement date

On the basis that you can retire at a date that works for you in a tax-efficient way, a number of factors should be considered, including the following:

- level of profits;
- level of overlap profits brought forward;
- new sources of income;
- tax rates; and
- timing of capital repayment.

These factors cannot be looked at in isolation, as they interact with each other. We have already seen in Example 4 that by bringing forward the retirement date by one month, partnership profits of £150,000 would suffer tax at 45% and you would be unable to utilise the 20% and 40% tax bands of the following year. That example did not take into account other sources of income and in particular any new sources of income – for example, pension income or future consultancy income – which could utilise the 20% and 40% tax bands in the following tax year and reduce the impact of bringing forward the retirement date.

If tax rates are changing, it may be tax efficient to bring forward or delay retirement as a result of the impact of the new tax rates coming into force. If a 50% tax rate were to be brought in from 6 April 2020, then bringing forward the retirement date could be tax efficient, as profits would be taxed at 45% rather than 50%.

The only way to reflect and consider appropriately is to work out the tax implications of different possible scenarios.

For example, following on from Examples 3 and 4 above, if pension income were £5,000 per month, the assessable income would be as detailed below.

Example 3A

	£
Taxable profits to 30 April 2020	360,000
Less overlap profits brought forward	(55,000)
11 months' pension income	55,000
Assessable income 2020/21	£360,000
Assessable income 2021/22	
12 months' pension income	£60,000

Example 4A

	£
Taxable profits to 30 April 2019	340,000
Taxable profits for the 11 months to 31 March 2020	330,000
Less overlap profits brought forward	(55,000)
Assessable income 2019/20	£615,000
Assessable income 2020/21	
12 months' pension income	£60,000

9. Tax reserves

This is the amount that the firm holds on your behalf in respect of your future tax liabilities. Every firm will have its own policy in this regard, and a retiring partner will need to find out what the firm's policy is and, in practical terms, what that means for him or her. A number of questions should be raised in connection with the tax liabilities that will be arising in the future.

9.1 What reserves does the firm retain?

For those firms with a 31 March year-end, a partner would expect sufficient tax reserves to be held to settle the tax on partnership income to the date that he or she retires.

"If tax rates are changing, it may be tax efficient to bring forward or delay retirement as a result of the impact of the new tax rates coming into force."

As ever, the situation is potentially more complex for firms with accounting year-end dates other than 31 March. There are potentially three different reserving policies.

(a) Minimum reserve

This is where the firm holds tax reserves in respect of the fiscal year only.

On this basis, on retirement, there is likely to be an under-reserve and the retiring partner will need to fund the tax liabilities arising in respect of the last tax year in which he or she was a partner.

(b) Retirement fund basis

Tax reserves are held taking into account the overlap profits. The reserves should match the tax liabilities and there should be no hidden surprises as to whether there are sufficient funds to settle the ongoing tax liabilities arising on partnership profits.

(c) Full tax reserves

Tax reserves are held ignoring overlap profits. The reserves will more than cover the tax liabilities, as overlap profits will not have been taken into account when calculating the tax reserves. There will be no hidden surprises in respect of whether there are sufficient funds to settle the tax liabilities leading up to retirement. Given that overlap profits have not been taken into account, there should be a net repayment due back to the partner.

Alternatively, some firms may operate a straight percentage basis and therefore there could be a potential shortfall in the tax reserves.

It is therefore key to establish whether sufficient tax reserves are held to settle future tax liabilities or whether there is a shortfall (and, if so, to what extent), so that plans can be made to ensure sufficient funds are available at the appropriate time to fund the payments.

Some questions that will need to be raised with the firm are as follows.

- **When will the firm release your tax reserves?** Will they be released automatically? Will you have to ask for them to be released?
- **How are they released?** Are your tax reserves held by the firm paid to you or directly to HMRC?
- **What tax do I need to pay personally?** A partner should expect to settle tax liabilities on personal income out of his or her own resources.

10. Self-assessment tax return

As a partner, you will have filed – or your tax adviser/accountant will have filed on your behalf – your annual UK self-assessment tax return in respect of the year ending 5 April.

To file a paper tax return, the deadline for submission is 31 October following the end of the tax year.

To file electronically, the deadline is 31 January following the end of the tax year.

If the return is late, penalties will be levied.

Delay	Penalty
Missed deadline	£100
3–6 months	Daily penalty £10 per day up to 90 days
6 months	£300 or 5% of the tax liability if higher
12 months*	£300 or 5% of the tax liability if higher

**If the tax return is 12 months late and the taxpayer deliberately withholds information, the penalty can be 100% of the tax liability or £300 if greater. A lower penalty may potentially be negotiated.*

10.1 Tax liabilities

While you were a partner, it is likely that the firm retained from your profit share sufficient funds to settle your tax liabilities on a timely basis. Once you retire, you are on your own and will have to ensure sufficient funds are put to one side for you to settle your future tax liabilities on a timely basis. Tax paid late will give rise to interest being levied by HMRC. Penalties will also be levied if tax liabilities for a tax year are paid later than 28 days after the due date.

Tax is effectively due in three instalments; this ignores any tax due under PAYE paid to the tax authorities by an employer.

There are two interim tax instalments for each tax year and then a final balancing payment. The interim instalments are payable on 31 January in the tax year and 31 July following the end of the tax year, with the balancing payment due the following 31 January. The interim instalments are 50% of the previous year's tax liability. There is scope to make reduction claims, although care is required: payments on account are based on total income for the year and a reduction claim may be required in anticipation of the first payment on account due on 31 January in the tax year.

"Once you retire, you are on your own and will have to ensure sufficient funds are put to one side for you to settle your future tax liabilities on a timely basis. Tax paid late will give rise to interest being levied by HMRC."

You will need to liaise with the firm to establish when you will be responsible for starting to pay your tax personally and what reserves it holds on your behalf.

Example 5: Your firm has a 31 March year-end and you are retiring on 31 March 2020, the first date on which a tax payment is due after your retirement will be 31 July 2020. Who is settling the liability? What is it for?

- **31 July 2020 | 2019/20 tax year | 2nd payment on account**
  If the firm has sufficient tax reserves and has not paid your tax reserves out to you, the expectation would be that the firm is responsible for liabilities arising on partnership income and you are responsible for liabilities arising on personal income.

- **31 January 2021 | 2019/20 tax year | Balancing payment**
  As before, if the firm has sufficient tax reserves and has not paid your tax reserves out to you, the expectation would be that the firm is responsible for liabilities arising on partnership income and you in respect of liabilities arising on personal income.

- **31 January 2021 | 2020/21 tax year | 1st payment on account**
  You will be paying – no partnership profits are assessable.

As the payment on account will be based on the 2019/20 tax liability, which was the last year in which you had partnership income, it is likely that a reduction claim will be necessary to bring the tax liability down to a realistic level.

Example 6: Your firm has a 30 April year-end and you are retiring on 30 April 2020. The first date on which a tax payment is due will be 31 July 2020. Who is settling the liability and future liabilities? What do the liabilities relate to?

- **31 July 2020 | 2019/20 tax year | 2nd payment on account**
  Based on profit share for the accounting year ending 30 April 2019.

  The firm is paying liabilities arising on partnership income, on the assumption that it has sufficient tax reserves and has not paid your tax reserves out to you. You will be responsible for liabilities arising on personal income.

- **31 January 2021 | 2019/20 tax year | Balancing payment**
  Based on profit share for the accounting year ending 30 April 2019.

  The firm is paying liabilities arising on partnership income, on the assumption that it has sufficient tax reserves and has not paid your tax reserves out to you. You will be responsible for liabilities arising on personal income.

- **31 January 2021 | 2020/21 tax year | 1st payment on account**
  Based on profit share for the accounting year ending 30 April 2020.

  The expectation would be that the firm is responsible in respect of liabilities arising on partnership income. This assumes that the firm has sufficient tax reserves and has not paid your tax reserves out to you.

  Any payment on account arising on personal income will be payable by you.

  A reduction claim may be appropriate in respect of net partnership profits after overlap relief. However, a reduction claim must be based on estimated total income; hence, an element of the payment on account may be in respect of personal income and you will thus be responsible for paying that element. You may need to pay a 'buffer' amount, to reduce the possibility of interest charges if the reduction claim proves to be excessive.

- **31 July 2021 | 2020/21 tax year | 2nd payment on account**
  Based on profit share for the accounting year ending 30 April 2020.

  The expectation would be that the firm is responsible in respect of liabilities arising on partnership income. This assumes that the firm has sufficient tax reserves and has not paid your tax reserves out to you.

  Any payment on account arising on personal income will be payable by you.

  This is an opportunity to reconsider whether a reduction claim is appropriate or whether a previous claim needs tweaking. You may need to pay a 'buffer' amount, to reduce the possibility of interest charges in the event that the reduction claim proves to be excessive.

  Revalidate how the payment on account is split between personal and partnership profits.

- **31 January 2022 | 2020/21 tax year | Balancing payment**
  Based on profit share for the accounting year ending 30 April 2020.

  The expectation would be that the firm is responsible in respect of liabilities arising on partnership income. This assumes that the firm has sufficient tax reserves and has not paid your tax reserves out to you.

  Any liabilities arising on personal income will be payable by you.

- **31 January 2022 | 2021/22 tax year | 1st payment on account**
  You are paying – no partnership profits assessable.

  As the payment on account will be based on the 2020/21 tax liability, which was the last year in which you had partnership income, it is likely that a reduction claim will be necessary to bring the tax liability down to a realistic level.

10.2 Interest on partnership capital loan

While a partner, tax (and NIC) relief is due on interest paid in respect of borrowings, to enable capital to be paid into the firm.

"To maximise tax relief on loan interest, advise the bank of your retirement in advance and arrange for interest to be charged up to the date of retirement."

Tax (and NIC) relief is not due on interest paid after you cease being a partner of the firm. This is the case even if the firm retains capital and repays it back to you over a period of time.

To maximise tax relief on loan interest, advise the bank of your retirement in advance and arrange for interest to be charged up to the date of retirement.

Tax relief on interest paid may be restricted where capital has been repaid to the partner and the funds have not been used to repay borrowings.

10.3 Selling your share of goodwill

Some firms will buy and sell goodwill when partners join and leave. This is treated as a capital transaction between connected parties and Statement of Practice D12 (SP D12) will need to be considered to work out the corresponding base cost and market value.

The net capital gain will be subject to capital gains tax (CGT).

Will entrepreneurs' relief (ER) be available to reduce the CGT rate to 10%? Certain criteria must be met for ER to apply. In broad terms, the partner must have held at least 5% interest in the firm during the whole of the last 24 months leading up to the date of retirement.

If ER does not apply, then the CGT rate (currently 20%) will apply.

10.4 Selling your shares in a service company

If a firm has a service company, some or all of the partners will be shareholders. The disposal of the shares when a partner retires will give rise to a capital transaction and a CGT liability if the proceeds/deemed proceeds are more than the capital gains annual exemption. A deemed proceeds rule will apply if the disposal is to a connected person, in which case market value will apply.

ER may be available, which will give rise to a CGT rate of 10%. Certain criteria must be met for ER to apply.

In essence, the criteria are as follows:

- The shares have been owned by the partner for at least 24 months immediately before the shares are disposed of.
- The company is a trading company.
- The partner is an officer of the company (ie, a director).
- The partner holds at least 5% of the ordinary share capital and voting rights.
- The partner is beneficially entitled to at least 5% of either:

- the profits and assets available for distribution on the winding up of the company; or
- the proceeds of the company had it been sold on the day of the disposal.

If ER does not apply, then the CGT rate of 20% will apply.

11. Post retirement

11.1 Annuities

In years gone by, it was not unusual for professional firms to provide an annuity instead of purchasing goodwill. If an annuity is payable, it is usually to a former partner for a fixed period or for the rest of his or her life, and perhaps for his or her spouse or dependants at a reduced rate for the rest of their lives. As people now live longer, interest rates have fallen and the level of the annuity is often attached to the performance of the firm, the level of profits required by a firm to maintain annuities has become unsustainable; hence, annuities are now commonly restricted in terms of both the level of payout and the period of payment.

As an annuity is usually to replace purchasing goodwill, there is the potential that CGT may arise. If the annuity is paid by a firm due to age or ill-health and is in reasonable recognition of past service, then under SP D12 (which provides details as to what is meant by reasonable recognition), CGT will not apply. For example, an annuity paid to an individual who was a partner for more than 10 years and is less than two-thirds of his or her average share of profits in the last seven years while working as a partner in a full-time capacity will not be subject to CGT.

If an annuity is paid and is in excess of reasonable recognition of past service, then the market value of the annuity will be treated as consideration for CGT purposes. ER may apply.

If an annuity is paid out to a former partner, it is crucial to gather the information detailed below, to assist with planning future income:

- the date on which the annuity will commence;
- the frequency of the annuity;
- the duration of the annuity; and,
- the level of the annuity.

Annuities will be subject to income tax and will form part of your total income.

Annuities paid to UK resident former partners will be paid after deduction of basic rate tax, currently 20%.

Depending on the level of total income, the former partner may need to make provision to settle future tax liabilities on the annuity income (ie, a further 20% or 25% on the grossed-up annuity received during the tax year, depending on the former partner's marginal rate of tax – 40% or 45%).

11.2 Directorships

A former partner may secure a directorship. As this role is an officer of the company, fees paid are subject to PAYE.

11.3 Consultancy

Former partners may negotiate a consultancy agreement with their former firm and/or with other entities. The question is whether the income from these consultancy contracts will be regarded as self-employed income or employment income. Moreover, will the work be carried out via a personal service company (PSC)? The options are as follows:

- Self-employment: Setting up your own advisory consultancy with a broad client base; working under a contract for services.
- Self-employment – acting as a 'consultant' to your old firm only; working under a contract for services.

"As people now live longer, interest rates have fallen and the level of the annuity is often attached to the performance of the firm, the level of profits required by a firm to maintain annuities has become unsustainable; hence, annuities are now commonly restricted in terms of both the level of payout and the period of payment."

- Employment: Performing services personally under a contract of service for your old firm, a new firm or as an office holder.
- PSC (or LLP): Operating via your PSC or LLP; working under a contract for services.

The benefits of self-employment include the ability to claim deductions for expenses wholly and exclusively for business purposes. Care must be taken in respect of travel costs and, in particular, private commuting costs and use of home expenses.

When you start a consultancy business, you must keep a watchful eye on your level of taxable supplies of services, to ensure that, if appropriate, you register for value added tax (VAT) at the appropriate time. If you exceed the compulsory VAT registration threshold in any rolling 12-month period, or if you expect to exceed the compulsory VAT registration threshold within the next 30 days, you must register for VAT and charge VAT.

You can voluntarily register for VAT at any time prior to reaching the VAT threshold. The advantage of doing so is that you can reclaim VAT on your purchases.

"When you start a consultancy business, you must keep a watchful eye on your level of taxable supplies of services, to ensure that, if appropriate, you register for value added tax (VAT) at the appropriate time."

Getting VAT wrong may result in liability for interest and penalties.

11.4 Self-employed or employed?

To establish whether you are self-employed or employed, several points must be considered, including the following:

- the right to substitute;
- the right of control;
- financial risk;
- mutuality of obligations;
- provision of own equipment;
- opportunity to profit;
- degree of integration into the business;
- the right to terminate the contract;
- the number of paymasters;
- business structure; and
- length of engagement.

The HMRC website has a Check Employment Status for Tax (CEST) indicator, which assists you in making a judgement as to your employment status.

The CEST indicator also assists in considering whether IR35 (a set of tax and NI rules) applies when you perform services for a client under an arrangement involving an intermediary – commonly a PSC (or perhaps a personal service LLP).

If IR35 is in point, then, for that particular assignment, income generated and tax and NICs will be applicable and payable by the PSC. This applies now for engagements with all private sector organisations, but from 6 April 2020 will apply only for engagements with 'small' entities which are not public sector bodies.

(a) Off-payroll rules

Under the new off-payroll rules, from 6 April 2020 engagers which are not small entities take over the responsibility for assessing the nature of the engagement and whether the person (the fee payer) paying the personal services intermediary should be deducting PAYE and NICs on payments made. The engager and fee payer can, but will not always, be the same organisation.

HMRC believes that the IR35 rules currently in place are not effective. Therefore, from 6 April 2020, private sector businesses will need to identify and review the employment status of all workers engaged through personal service intermediaries and treat them as deemed employees for tax and NIC purposes.

In light of these new rules, a partner who is considering setting up a consultancy business post-retirement should plan how to work for businesses.

(b) Protecting your pension lifetime allowance

If you have protected your lifetime allowance, then you cannot make future pension contributions from the date on which you made the election. Any subsequent pension contributions made will invalidate the election.

However, it is normal when working as an employee to be automatically enrolled into your employer's workplace pension scheme. You will have a short window of one month to opt out from the scheme; this normally lasts three years before the employer is required to automatically enrol you again and you will again need to opt out.

There are many technical tax issues to consider when you plan for retirement.

V. The emotional impact of partner retirement

Micheline Hogan
Psychodynamic psychotherapist

1. Introduction

The legal profession is justifiably renowned for thoughtful preparation, detailed analysis and careful attempts to anticipate all contingencies. However, for many partners in law firms, there is little evidence of these qualities being put to use when planning for their own personal circumstances. Typically, some partners come under psychological pressure in two situations. The first is when their firm imposes retirement on them, contrary to their wishes. The second is when they are simply not prepared for the change in responsibility and status that accompanies retirement.

This chapter explores the use of psychoanalytic thinking, as well as the different strategies that could be employed to facilitate the retirement process and mitigate some of these difficulties. It also sets out further recommendations on how to go about seeking help for those partners who are struggling to embrace retirement.

Retirement is "the withdrawal from one's position or occupation or from one's active working life". Most law firms have rules of some kind regarding partners' retirement from the business: some firms have different rules pertaining to different levels of seniority; some offer partners more flexibility than others. In one scenario, a principal may choose to retire at any stage between the ages 60 to 65, or may choose to go on even longer. In a second scenario, an equity partner may be required by a clause in the partnership agreement to retire at a specific age – often 65, reflecting the age when traditionally state pension benefits became payable. In a third scenario, some firms offer gradual and flexible retirement by allowing partners to undertake consultancy work or to work in a less demanding position.

Partners in law firms bear heavy responsibilities (including managing employees, generating income for the law firm and ensuring compliance with wide-ranging legal and professional rules). While some of these responsibilities apply to any senior manager of a business, some apply specifically to the practice of law and so circumstances surrounding the retirement of lawyers must take a particular approach.

2. Plan in advance

For those who feel unprepared for this next stage of life, it is worth establishing a well-thought-out plan in advance, in order for the process to be a success. It is no different from any other major life change that requires detailed and considered decision making. Becoming a partner in a law firm does not happen overnight: there are certain criteria to meet and a planned trajectory to reach that rank. Retiring is no different; it should be viewed and treated as a time for personal growth.

To begin with, initiating open discussions with one's firm about potential timescales for retirement is important. Negotiate a plan that will work for both parties, with the mutual goal of ensuring a smooth and successful handover of clients and responsibilities. Part of the planning process is also to be upfront with clients and recommend a transfer to another colleague within the team. Being transparent with them will evoke reassurance that they are in good hands and will ease the process of letting go.

Additionally, past and present colleagues and friends who themselves have gone through or are approaching retirement can be vital sounding boards and a source of comfort. Establishing regular meetings will help to create a space to contemplate life outside work and develop a forum for reflecting on strengths and weaknesses, as well as the sharing of ideas and airing of concerns, such as future financial implications or health insurance queries. Seeking out those who are already retired (from all professions, not just the law) and who are genuinely settled into their next phase can only be beneficial. Be inquisitive regarding the changes they have made in their lives: ask specifically what their new activities are and how these replaced and compensated for the rhythms of working life. Inquire which paths were satisfying and which were not. Be encouraged to approach anyone who appeals to you as a source of reference and guidance. These encounters will help you to imagine and mould a new post-work life structure; going forward, they will also help you to monitor progress or – equally important – expose any struggles that might arise when establishing practical plans. These gatherings should be viewed as a meeting of minds and a joint effort for self-improvement.

Crucially, these bridge-building conversations may help to identify at an early stage the potential causes behind any dilemmas. For example, one theme might be: where will I obtain the sort of stimulation to which I am accustomed? While it is likely that there may be no immediate answers to this question, this process should generate ideas or potential paths during the sharing process. Openly discussing these concerns not only makes them significantly more manageable, but also helps to normalise the fact that many others have wrestled with these concepts.

3. Alternative strategies

Other meaningful strategies to consider include gradually scaling down working hours to experience life outside work and focusing on a weekly activity that may have previously been overlooked. Make a point of achieving and maintaining consistent working hours by

"Initiating open discussions with one's firm about potential timescales for retirement is important. Negotiate a plan that will work for both parties, with the mutual goal of ensuring a smooth and successful handover of clients and responsibilities."

"Make a point of achieving and maintaining consistent working hours by putting a predictable structure around the transition period and delegating anything outstanding to younger partners."

putting a predictable structure around the transition period and delegating anything outstanding to younger partners. This will speed up their learning curve and offer opportunities for the exiting partner to be available to provide internal counsel while still present. Ideally – although this may not be feasible in all firms – winding down over a six-month period is the optimum timeframe.

Planning a farewell party is also an important strategy, as well as fun, as it facilitates closure. Leaving on a positive note is important, as this provides retired partners with the platform to receive appreciation for their hard work and contribution to the firm. Additionally, lining up a holiday with family or friends soon after concluding work will help to disconnect with office life and allow the immediate feeling of freedom that comes with retirement. It draws a tangible line under the transition and gives a taste of what is to come when one retires: quality time with family and friends.

When speaking to partners who have settled into retirement, most revealed that they never looked back. They were ready to let go of their demanding role. As expected, they still acknowledged that they missed the stimulating meetings, interactions with colleagues and clients, but stated that they didn't miss the stress that came with their responsibilities. They further indicated that they were satisfied with their achievements and ready to pass on the torch to the next generation of partners. They recognised that getting help from their law firm to plan their next steps or having the choice of when to retire facilitated this process. They had come to enjoy the freedom that retirement brings and were able finally to fully engage in activities or hobbies that were not possible while holding such a demanding role.

Additionally, these partners spoke of the enjoyment that came with having more opportunity to travel. One commented that she was finally able to go to some parts of the world that she had previously been unable to consider because of the limited amount of holiday she could take while working. Another said that he could not remember going on holiday without being disrupted by emails or calls from colleagues and clients. Most recalled the joy of having time to invest in their health by boosting their energy through engaging in a range of physical activities, such as going to the gym, swimming, joining a cycling group or playing golf. Another outlined the health benefits gained through practising mindfulness, explaining that when she retired, she struggled to settle down as she was so used to being continuously on the go that she had never known how to relax. The daily breathing techniques embedded in mindfulness helped her to learn to live more in the moment and became instrumental in allowing her to appreciate each of her regular activities, to be less reactive and more in touch with her body; this all contributed significantly to her general sense of wellbeing.

Aside from travel and exercise, there are myriad other ways to redefine oneself after a long working life. Being able to indulge in a passion or hobby has extremely positive ramifications, and embracing life without work – perhaps learning about the art world, taking up a musical instrument or beginning to paint or draw – is a valuable use of time. I recently heard from a partner the delight he gained from being taught piano by his granddaughter. A colleague mentioned that her husband was going back to university to do a degree in music, as he eventually wants to become a conductor. One partner had decided to pass on her experience and expertise by stepping into teaching; another had been teaching English to children in deprived areas of London as his way of giving back to society.

These examples are encouraging to prospective retirees. However, it should not be underestimated that the onset of retirement inevitably comes with losses: self-image, prestige, interaction, daily structure and a sense of belonging – the experience is bound to cause conflicting emotions. And while some partners – with the support of their firm, family and friends, and solid planning – have managed to navigate their way through these difficult emotions, for others this can trigger an identity crisis and a lack of self-worth. Some can feel completely lost as they embark into uncharted territory. It is my experience as a psychotherapist that the cause of this is often insufficient preparation stemming from the lack of support from their law firms.

4. Defining your post-retirement role

Retiring partners often feel so defined by what they do that they can't think of themselves in any capacity other than as a partner. Their lives can feel empty as they have never really had much of a chance to experience things outside work and might have a sparse social life. These individuals generally feel guilty at enjoying themselves or having free time, and often regret not having previously joined in any extracurricular activities with their spouse or children. They often question their self-worth, worrying how they will be perceived by society and fearing that they will be considered as insignificant once they have finished working. Those individuals who encounter difficulties working through the emotions that come with retirement often feel this way not just about the loss of their work life, but also about past losses in their personal life which they have not yet been able to work through. It is my contention that work is often used as a shield to keep deeply painful feelings at bay; yet they now resurface, triggered by the onset of retirement. It is the psychoanalytic thinking that with loss comes mourning; and unless these losses have been mourned properly and worked through, this will prevent creativity and curiosity from taking shape and it won't be possible to gain pleasure from other aspects of life.

One partner I observed really struggled with his retirement as a result of being forced into it and having not been adequately prepared. He felt bereft at the disappearance of a daily structure. He felt let down by his firm and thought it was unfair to have had to end his career at that time, as he thought he was in fairly good health and still had much to contribute. He expressed regret at having given so much of his life to the firm only to feel unsupported when it was time for him to leave. Moreover, he felt lost as he had very few hobbies or and no real social life to throw himself into; he did not know what to do with himself now that he had so much free time. He was divorced and had grown-up children who had their own life. The grief that he experienced from his divorce left him feeling low, with a sense of emptiness and isolation. When I inquired about his divorce, he revealed that it had been acrimonious, especially with regard to the custody of the children. In hindsight, he acknowledged that he was not around much as a result of his demanding work schedule. There was no doubt in my mind that work had become a defence against deep-rooted, painful feelings of regret, emptiness and guilt as a result of his divorce, as well as the inability to see his children as often he wanted to. The onset of retirement triggered the deep emotional responses that he was experiencing.

"Retiring partners often feel so defined by what they do that they can't think of themselves in any capacity other than as a partner."

Once I made him aware of the roots of his depressive anxiety, working through the painful feelings of his divorce and the loss of his former self, things started to shift. He was able to reflect on his actions and became proactive in setting goals for himself. For instance, one of his choices was to start regularly picking up his grandson from school – something he had been unable to do with his own children because of his all-encompassing work life. When he described his symptoms of feeling isolated, I suggested that it would be good for him to join a walking group, as it would lift his mood and help him to feel less alone. Initially, he was not at all keen, telling me that he was not a fan of walking; but in the end, he decided to try it. After a few meetings, he mentioned how much he enjoyed walking and talking with the other members of the group.

At one session, he arrived and announced with great enthusiasm that he was going to enrol on a garden design course. I inquired as to what had prompted him to make that decision and he told me that the previous week he had been to Blenheim Palace with the walking group and had enjoyed exploring the garden; he now wanted to learn more about the various plants, trees and flowers. I observed that he had started to see the bright side of retirement. He had found a new purpose in his life and as a result his mood shifted.

"Retirement is, in principle, a withdrawal from one's professional position; but it is not a reduction of one's innate abilities. It is merely an opportunity to refocus attention on what may still be achieved and enjoyed in life."

We held a few more meetings and he continued to be proactive in making further plans to travel around the country discovering public gardens with members of the group, and establishing new friendships along the way. He thought that since he was in fairly good health, he wanted to give back to the community and was making inquiries with various gardening associations to do some volunteering one day a week to plant areas in his local community. This was his way of pursuing his new-found passion and feeling needed. He also mentioned that he was approached by a start-up company which was seeking a legal resource to handle some consulting work for them. He agreed to do it, as he felt he still had a lot to offer and was sufficiently active enough to potentially source new streams of income through this route, which eased his financial uncertainty. He further revealed that he felt useful because his experience was still relevant and needed by the next generation.

In this particular case, once the individual had the chance to mourn and work through difficult moments of his past (his divorce) as well as his present losses (retirement), he was able to reflect not only on what he had achieved, but also on what he had missed out on by dedicating himself to his work. In becoming curious about other hobbies, he was able to reinvent himself and find a new purpose in life, which ultimately created a sense of belonging and validation.

5. Concluding thoughts

Retirement should be a time of enjoyment, and it can be if one is able to prepare well in advance and have a structure in place by the time it happens. Retirement is, in principle, a withdrawal from one's professional position; but it is not a reduction of one's innate abilities. It is merely an opportunity to refocus attention on what may still be achieved and enjoyed in life. This is a point when one may freely fulfil any needs and desires that have previously been left disregarded. The phase following work life can broaden horizons in many satisfying means or forms. Acquired knowledge and professional experiences remain relevant and valuable – not only as a pillar of post-retirement life, but also with the gratification that comes with sharing experiences and learning with the next generation. For those who find retirement challenging and may be embarrassed that, as a result of social expectations, they don't find the notion of finishing work inherently enjoyable, it is imperative that they confide in family members or friends, so as to not to struggle and suffer in silence.

An effective place to start for those partners who feel unprepared or daunted by the prospect of freedom that accompanies retirement is a few sessions with a coach. Through this, they can get the support they need to navigate their path clearly. As for those who are emotionally destabilised by the onset of retirement, it is crucial that they reach out to healthcare professionals such as their GP or a trained and accredited therapist for support. This will facilitate gaining an understanding of the root causes underlying any emotional turmoil, which can only be to the benefit of the partner and those around him or her. Failing to seek help may result in physical illnesses and/or mental health problems such as depression, or may even bring about dependencies on alcohol or other substances as an emotional crutch.

Life is made up of seasons. For all partners, irrespective of their outlook, retirement is a key milestone within the cycle. It is ultimately each partner's individual choice on how best to embrace this major change to construct a satisfying, meaningful and contented existence for the days ahead. Early preparation, awareness of the emotional impact and willingness to seek guidance are the cornerstones of that process.

VI. Financial aspects of retirement planning: a 10-point retirement plan

Veronica Mann
Talis Financial Advisers

1. Make your plan

When you go on holiday, you probably spend a long time deciding on when and where to go and how to get there. Your retirement is the longest 'holiday' of your life, so it deserves at least as much attention.

Have you ever really thought about what you want to do in retirement? Retirement is not a destination; it is merely another step in your journey. A number of people have told me that they plan to retire at 60 or 65; but when asked "Why?", they do not have an answer. If that is the end of the journey, as far as you can see, you may not have a happy, productive and fulfilling retirement. The future could look rather bleak unless you spend some time thinking about what retirement means to you.

So: what do you want to do in retirement? Will you stop work entirely or gradually wind down? Do you have a target age in mind? How will you use your time? Do you want to travel, explore the world, study or spend more time with family and friends? Have you any hobbies? Will you start something new? Even golf fanatics find that they cannot play seven days a week and still enjoy it. While you have your health, you need to plan to do as many of the things that you can possibly enjoy before old age or illness prevents you from doing so.

You also need to think about your family. How old will your spouse or partner be when you retire? Does he or she want to retire at the same time? If so, you can decide how to use your time together or separately. However, if he or she is not ready to retire, then how will you handle that?

How much money will you need? Income requirements in retirement will change. Retirement tends to go in phases. During the early years, people are active, as work is replaced with leisure, travel, hobbies and so on. As time passes, activities may decrease. In later years, you may find that activities diminish further due to health or physical limitations; but other costs may increase, such as heating or care support; and finally, you may be 'on your own' after losing a spouse or partner. How you create and draw your income should allow for these variations.

Why do you go to work? And why would you want to stop? Most people go to work to generate the money that they need to fund their lifestyle. Most people want to stop when they have had enough of work, have made enough money to stop or are required to stop due to ill health.

What is the most important thing to you in your retirement? I asked my top 20 clients this question and the answer came back, 'financial security'. But what did they mean? Is it just having 'enough'? If so, I could probably show you how to have financial security right now. Simply sell your home, chattels, car, jewellery – anything that has value – and buy a cheap flight to somewhere like Butuan City in the Philippines – a modern, thriving city, where your money will go twice as far. Or perhaps to a village such as Barangay Lajala on Uson island, where people live in modest bamboo homes and the main income is from fishing. You will now be financially secure!

But will you be happy? Will you miss your friends, family, culture? In reality, most people don't want financial security – they want to protect their lifestyle. This is the most important priority, after your health. And to do this, you need to know what your 'number' is – that is, how much you will need at any particular time, so that you can do what you want to do, when you want to do it, without fear of ever running out of money.

How will you find your 'number'? This is constructed from your own expenses and spending, both now and in the future. Spending habits change in retirement. Even just staying at home can cost more, with increased heating or grocery bills and additional costs of leisure activities to make sure you're not bored. Some do spend less. Download a planning template from www.london-ifa.net/personal.

"In reality, most people don't want financial security – they want to protect their lifestyle."

This can help you to consider how your 'number' might alter as your life changes. It lets you think about what you need, both pre-retirement and post-retirement, and should you find yourself on your own.

You also need to consider the many 'What ifs...?' What if the markets fall when you need funds? What if your health fails and you need to provide for care costs? What if your children need money? And how will your own appetite for risk change as time passes?

Your planning will revolve around an 'age' – the date you have targeted when you will stop work; but it can be very hard to stick to this. Retirement is a massive change and sometimes it is easier to continue with the 'known', which means not retiring. Knowing that you can afford to retire – that you have 'enough' – will afford you that peace of mind to help you make that change.

With a business plan, you can see how to develop your business and how to keep on track, and spot where things are working and where they are not. Do you have the personal equivalent – a personal financial plan? Without one, how will you know what you can (and can't) do, and when you can do it?

A professional lifetime inflation-adjusted cash-flow forecast could be your personal plan. It will let you model different scenarios, such as what will happen if you don't – or can't – retire at the age you have chosen; whether you will have enough if you need to pay for care; whether you can afford to gift to your children or to charity without fear of running out of money. It will look at tax breaks and tax traps.

Life is not a rehearsal. We don't get second chances and you need to make the best of your life. You can't delay your planning, because accidents happen. Now is a great time to put your house in order.

2. Where will it come from?

2.1 Pensions

You have several ways to create the value you need to achieve your 'number', including the sale of your business; but when people think of retirement, their first thoughts tend to involve pensions. A pension is simply a savings plan with special tax benefits and rules. Over the years, there have been myriad different pensions, all with different rules. You could have one or several types.

The advantages of pension saving include the following:

"Life is not a rehearsal. We don't get second chances and you need to make the best of your life. You can't delay your planning, because accidents happen. Now is a great time to put your house in order."

- Contributions are made net of basic rate tax.
- Contributions receive tax relief at your highest marginal rate.
- You or your company/employer can contribute to a plan.
- The funds grow in a tax-favourable environment.
- A tax-free lump sum of 25% of the fund can be taken once you reach the age of 55 (in most cases).
- The funds are exempt from inheritance tax (in most cases).

Pensions were meant to replace your income when you stopped work. The facility to draw 100% of your pension from age 55 only became available in 2015. Previously, people did not really consider pension funds to be 'their' money, as they usually had to buy an annuity with the funds. You could not necessarily go to your pension and withdraw £30,000 to buy a new car. If you died the day after purchasing an annuity, the money was spent and gone, unless you had included a widow's pension or protection.

The state pension was introduced in January 1909. It was paid to men over the age of 70 at a rate of five shillings a week and was means tested. At that time, only around one in four reached the age of 70. We have moved a long way since then.

The basic state pension for those reaching state pension age after April 2016 is £8,767.20 per annum (2019/20). Entitlement to state pension depends on your national insurance contributions (NICs), so you may not receive the maximum. NICs are paid for you, if employed, via your employer; alternatively, you pay Class 2 contributions if self-employed. You need 35 qualifying years to receive the maximum pension and you can buy extra years. You can find out what this would cost at www.gov.uk.

There have been three different schemes to boost the basic state pension and your entitlement could include any of them:

- the Graduated Pension Scheme;
- the State Earnings Related Pension Scheme; and
- the state second pension.

The state pension continues to change. You can check when you can draw your state pension and what your total benefit will be at www.gov.uk/check-state-pension.

This is an important 'number' to include in your planning, as it is guaranteed and currently inflation linked.

(a) Contributions

You can contribute up to £40,000 or 100% of your salary/net relevant earnings, whichever is the lower, in any tax year and receive tax relief at your highest marginal rate. If your 'adjusted' income (ie, income plus employer pension contributions) is more than £150,000, the £40,000 reduces on a sliding scale down to £10,000. The tapered reduction does not apply to those with threshold income (ie, income less personal pension contributions) of less than £110,000. If you have been a member of a pension scheme in the previous three years and have not used your full allowance, you may be able to make additional contributions to mop it up.

Personal contributions receive basic rate tax relief. A personal contribution of £800 becomes £1,000 inside your pension. If you are a higher-rate taxpayer, you can claim a further 20% or 25% through your self-assessment return, so putting £1,000 into a pension might only 'cost' you £550.

(b) Limitations

The money purchase lifetime allowance restricts the amount that an individual may amass in pension funds without incurring a tax charge. For the 2019/20 tax year, this is £1,055,000. If exceeded, the excess could be subject to a tax of 55% (depending on how the funds are accessed). The limit was initially £1.8 million and protection was available as the limit reduced. The lifetime allowance applies to the sum of all your pensions, including defined benefit pensions, but not your state pension. If you are approaching or have already exceeded this limit, you will want to be concerned about how the tax charge will affect you and how else you could save for your retirement.

(c) Defined contribution or money purchase plans

These are the most common types of pension schemes. The value of your benefits on retirement depends on the contributions paid, how long the money has been invested, the charges and investment returns over the period. That value is the amount that you can use, in accordance with pension scheme and tax rules. There are a number of different types of defined contribution plans, as discussed below.

Personal/private pensions: You can pay into a personal pension if you are employed, self-employed or even not working. You can contribute to more than one pension plan during the year, but your tax-effective contribution is limited (see above).

Self-invested personal pensions (SIPP): This affords a wider investment choice, including direct equities (stocks and shares) and commercial property.

Retirement annuity contracts or Section 226 contracts/pensions (pre-1998): These offered a potentially higher tax-free cash sum and guaranteed annuity rates.

Company pensions offered by employer (up to 6 April 2012): These include:

- contracted-out money purchase schemes, which allowed you to divert some of your NICs to your own personal pension (your contracting out history will impact on how much state pension you get); and
- contracted-in money purchase schemes.

Group personal pension plans: These are personal pensions offered via your employer. You own your own plan and can make individual investment choices. They are likely to have low ongoing charges, but may not offer full flexibility on retirement.

Stakeholder plans: These were the government's first attempt to persuade everyone to make provision for retirement by requiring employers to offer pensions to their employees. They are personal pensions with capped charges and many have limited fund choice. Your retirement benefits depend on the scheme rules, which may not include the new flexible regime.

Auto-enrolment: Most UK employers must now offer a workplace

"The value of your benefits on retirement depends on the contributions paid, how long the money has been invested, the charges and investment returns over the period."

pension plan and auto-enrol all their 'qualifying workers' into it with minimum contribution levels.

Small self-administered schemes (SSASs): These are for the benefit of directors and senior employees or partners. An SSAS can invest in the company, borrow money subject to terms and conditions for investment purposes (eg, raise a mortgage to allow the purchase of company premises) and even lend money to the company, which a SIPP cannot. If you are a member of an SSAS, you will need specialised advice as to how to draw funds when you reach retirement.

(d) Defined benefit or final salary schemes

These are offered by employers such as the NHS and local government and some larger private companies. They are controlled by the scheme rules – including a 'normal' retirement age with a guaranteed income, governed by the number of years for which you were employed and your pensionable salary at the date of leaving. They usually provide a widow's or dependants' pension and/or a lump sum in the event of your death. These plans are underwritten by the employer and benefit from a 'lifeboat' if the employer cannot meet its obligations. Prior to retirement, you can switch the funds into a personal pension to access the flexibility of the current pensions regime. The benefit of the guaranteed income can be very valuable and it is now compulsory to obtain financial advice if considering transferring out.

(e) Accessing pension funds on retirement

If you are in a defined benefit scheme, the pension administrators will send you a statement advising you of your benefits. You may be able to adjust the amount of tax-free cash and income, but you are limited by the scheme rules and actuarial calculations of the plan. If you are in a modern pension contract, you will have more choice, but no guarantees, including the following:

- Buying an annuity with all or some of the money: An annuity is a taxable income for life. You can buy one providing for a level or increasing income and can include your spouse, but no one else. You can select guaranteed annuities or investment-linked annuities, where the income could vary. You may be eligible for a higher annuity rate if your health is poor or have ever smoked. The rate offered by your pension provider may not be the best, so you need to check the market if you want to include an annuity in your retirement strategy.
- Flexible drawdown: This allows you to take income as and when you want it. You can draw 25% of the pension fund as a tax-free cash payment – the balance is taxable as income. Today, this allows you to pass any funds remaining on your death to anyone you nominate as a beneficiary. If you die before reaching 75, this

"The rate offered by your pension provider may not be the best, so you need to check the market if you want to include an annuity in your retirement strategy."

will be free of inheritance tax and income tax. However, you may run out of pension if you take more out than your fund can support.

2.2 Other assets

(a) Partnership/business

The value of your partnership or business may well form part of your retirement plan, either via sale value or an ongoing income stream for a period. This asset is exempt from inheritance tax, as it should qualify for business property relief (BPR). Once that sum reaches your bank account, not only must it be invested for your retirement, but it will also increase your inheritance tax liability unless appropriate investments are made.

(b) Property

Rental properties: You may have investment properties that generate rental income. Rental income is not guaranteed and both the income and any gain you make on sale are taxable. With the changes in landlord taxation, many people are finding that the figures no longer work for them and are looking to sell. Selling will create a capital gains tax (CGT) liability, which from 6 April 2020 must be paid within 30 days of the sale. You then need to reinvest the proceeds to fit in with your plans.

Your home: The home that you have been living in while you were working and bringing up your family may no longer be suitable for you as you grow older. It could be far too big, or have too many stairs or a garden that is too large to manage. You can release equity by downsizing. There is no CGT on selling your own home. Moving home at any time is one of the most stressful things you can do. Sorting through which possessions to keep or will fit in a smaller space after 20 or 30 years in the same house will take some time. Bear this in mind, as it becomes harder to do as you get older.

If you want to stay in your home, you could use a lifetime mortgage (equity release). This is a loan secured on your property. It is based on the value of the property, not your income, and can provide additional funds for your retirement. The loan need not be repaid until the property is sold or empty for six months or more. It will impact on any legacy you hope to leave, so you should involve your family in these decisions. Equity release lenders should be selected carefully, to get the best rate for you and your circumstances; make sure they have signed up to the Safe Home Income Plan Regulations which protect you from negative equity, among other things.

(c) Stocks and shares

Equities: Companies need to invest in their business to grow and will thus sell part of their business as shares/equities. These are traded on stock markets. The price fluctuates, varying with market sentiment and supply and demand. You can make money from shares either through capital growth or through any dividend income payments. Both are subject to CGT or dividend income tax, unless held within an individual savings account (ISA). Holding a narrow portfolio of shares is a high-risk strategy, as you may not have diversification or have too many 'eggs in one basket'.

ISAs: These offer tax-free growth and income. You have an annual personal allowance of £20,000 to invest. The choice is wide, from cash to collectives and equities. You can have ISAs with different companies and use different strategies, but you can only invest in one cash ISA and one stocks and shares ISA within the allowance in any tax year. These form part of your estate, unless held within an AIM ISA account, when they may be eligible for BPR.

Collective accounts (eg, unit trusts/investment trusts/exchange traded funds): An investment fund manager pools your money with money from other investors to purchase securities/stocks and shares. The fund manager will have a remit governing the investment strategy and permitted asset classes. One unit/share will be invested in many companies, usually between 20 and 50.

Other assets: You might have a collection of art or antiques which you plan to realise during your retirement. Generally, these are liable to CGT on the profit. An exception is something considered to be a 'wasting' chattel, where any gain is exempt. A surprising example is fine wine. Other chattels are exempt from CGT if the sale proceeds are below £6,000. You might like to consult an accountant so that you do not overpay this tax.

Venture capital trusts (VCTs): Successive governments have tried to encourage investors to invest in small or early-phase UK businesses. These are either unquoted or listed on the AIM market and considered to be riskier than larger, more established companies. The encouragement comes via a 30% income tax credit on investments of up to £200,000 (2019/20), if you buy shares in a new venture capital trust provided that you have paid enough tax to match the rebate. There is no tax on any dividends received and no CGT when you sell a VCT. You need to hold the shares for a minimum of five years to keep the tax breaks.

Enterprise investment schemes (EIS): These are government-sponsored, tax-advantaged investments designed to encourage investment in small unquoted companies. However, the rules

"Equity release lenders should be selected carefully, to get the best rate for you and your circumstances; make sure they have signed up to the Safe Home Income Plan Regulations which protect you from negative equity."

governing which companies can be included within an EIS and the tax advantages are different. Qualifying investors can receive income tax relief of 30% on the investment which can be carried back one year. There is a CGT exemption on profits on the sale, provided that the EIS has been held for a minimum of three years. An EIS falls within the BPR rules and so is currently exempt from inheritance tax, provided that shares are held for two years.

It is complicated to work out the best way to optimise these pieces in line with your own risk profile and create your retirement jigsaw picture. Getting it right will maximise your tax-free income, which means that your money should last longer, giving you more peace of mind.

3. Investment risk

There is no such thing as a 'no-risk' investment. You will always take on some risk when you invest. The degree varies between different types of investment. For example, money held in secure bank accounts is deemed to be 'safe'; but you are exposed to inflation risk. With the Consumer Price Index hovering around 2% over the last few years and a return of 0.5% to 1% (taxable), you have guaranteed yourself a loss of 1% to 1.5% per annum. So, while you need some money easily accessible for day to day and emergencies, you do not want to hold too much in cash.

You could also be exposed to:

- market risk – when the market drops as a whole, as in a recession;
- liquidity risk – you may be unable to sell your investment when you need to, which is particularly relevant in the case of property;
- concentration risk – if you have too many eggs in one basket and that basket breaks;
- timing risks – when the value of your investment drops without enough time to recover before you need the money; and
- sequence of returns risk – this is particularly important during retirement. If markets crash immediately after you start to take income, funds will be drawn from a reduced asset and larger returns will be needed to recover.

For example, if £1,000 were providing 5% per annum income, £50 could be withdrawn each year without capital erosion. If there were zero growth and £50 were withdrawn, the fund would have to grow by 5.26% to return to £1,000. A further 5% growth would be required to provide next year's income. The timing of withdrawals is therefore very important.

"There is no such thing as a 'no-risk' investment. You will always take on some risk when you invest."

3.1 Managing and minimising investment risk

- Diversification: In other words, buying shares in an umbrella factory and an ice cream factory. The profit cycle of both should provide an average return. Also, investing in different countries.
- Pound cost averaging: Making regular contributions can help to smooth out the highs and lows of the market and cut the risk of big losses.
- Long-term investing: You can generally afford to take more risk with investments that you don't need in the near future, as if there is a market downturn, you will hopefully have the time to make adjustments or for the fund to recover.

4. There's no point planning if disaster strikes...

This should really be the first piece of your jigsaw. You hope to have a long and healthy retirement, enjoying life with friends and family. Unfortunately, 'stuff' can happen at any time. It is prudent to create a safety net so that neither you nor your family suffer financially if that happens.

Your family are relying on you, though your working life and beyond, to provide funds for everything from the grocery bills upwards. Would they be able to manage if you were to die today or if you became unable to work? If you have any doubt, you should put some plans in place now. If you are a salaried partner/employed, you could use a relevant life plan to provide 'cheaper' tax-efficient life cover. The alternative is a simple life insurance plan to provide your family with the security that they need to protect their home and to live on in the event of your death.

What will happen if you can't work because of an illness or accident? How will you manage? You can't rely on the state. The initial support is £73.10 a week (2019/20) or £114.85 as a couple, and is subject to assessment by the Department of Work and Pensions. Apart from the issues in getting this payment, could you cope if that was all you had? You can provide your own bespoke protection to cover your specific needs and safeguard your family's home and lifestyle. You could create a regular income (income protection) or a lump-sum payment (critical illness plan) to clear the mortgage or to modify your home so you that you could still live there if disabled. Should you investigate this?

5. Legacy planning

Do you want to be able to leave a legacy? This need not necessarily be a financial one: you may want to help your community or those less well off, now that you have enough time to do so. In a perfectly executed plan, you might wish to die with just £10 in the bank; but

"You must always remember that you need to finance your own lifestyle. You must be cautious how much you give away and how you do it."

since you are planning to be able to do everything you want and never run out of money, you are likely to die with assets, which will be subject to inheritance tax.

5.1 Inheritance tax

You have paid tax on everything during your lifetime and your estate will be taxed on your death at 40%. Would you prefer to mitigate inheritance tax and pass more to your beneficiaries instead of the chancellor of the exchequer? There are allowances and options.

Everyone has a nil rate band: the first £325,000 of assets attracts a 0% rate of tax. You may also have a residential nil rate band, provided that you leave your home to your direct descendants – your children or grandchildren – and the net value of your estate is less than £2 million. This will be £175,000 in 2020/21, thereby creating a potential nil rate of £500,000. This is transferable between spouses and registered civil partners, so a couple could have a £1 million exemption.

There are other exemptions you can use during your lifetime. The main ones are an annual gift of £3,000 and regular gifts from income of any amount, provided that they do not impact on your normal standard of living. Larger gifts become exempt if made at least seven years before you die.

You must always remember that you need to finance your own lifestyle. You must be cautious how much you give away and how you do it. If you make a gift to your children – for example, a second home – but continue to use it, the chances are that HMRC will ignore the gift and include it within your taxable estate. For the gift to be ignored for inheritance tax purposes, the donor must give up all rights to it (ie, be excluded as a beneficiary).

One of your most favourable holdings is your pension. Most pensions are outside of the estate for inheritance tax calculations and may be passed tax free on your death, depending on the age at which you die. Which is one reason to spend your other assets first!

You could gift money into trust. A trust is a financial instrument through which trustees, appointed by the settlor/donor (ie, you), manage the assets in the trust on behalf of the beneficiaries (ie, the people who could receive the value). This is a potentially exempt transfer: no inheritance tax is due on making the gift and it will fall out of your estate after seven years. If you die within seven years, and only if the gift was more than the nil rate band, a tapering relief applies after three years.

You could use inheritance tax-friendly investments, which benefit from

"A partner who was not married to, or in a civil partnership with, the deceased has no automatic right to inherit."

BPR and so could be outside of your estate for inheritance tax after two years. You can still use those funds, but they are invested in higher-risk strategies and will not be suitable for everyone.

Some people know they have more than enough for now and would like to avoid inheritance tax, but are worried about the impact of care fees and prefer a lower risk profile.

A specific 'rolling' trust strategy allows you to benefit from the seven-year rule and have access to the funds on an annual basis. You can choose funds in line with your risk profile and objectives. This means that you can use the funds for care fees if they arise, or to cover education costs for grandchildren or make gifts to your own children.

Inheritance tax will leave your estate with at least £325,000, being the basic nil rate band. The cost of care fees could use up all bar £14,250 (England and Northern Ireland). Different limits apply in Scotland and Wales.

5.2 Care fees

There is very little aid from the state if you need extra help, unless you qualify for continuing healthcare or NHS-funded nursing care. Otherwise, the state will not help until your personal assets drop to

£23,250 (England and Northern Ireland). You can protect your estate from the impact of long-term care costs using an immediate needs annuity, but only once you need the care. This is paid directly to your care provider and is not taxed in your hands, making it cost effective. There is no longer any insurance that you can buy ahead of time. You could also consider a lifetime mortgage to provide the funds in this scenario.

Specialised financial planning help can be invaluable. Financial advisers must have extra qualifications to advise in these areas.

5.3 Wills and lasting power of attorney

Write a will. If you die without a valid will, the rules of intestacy will take over and your assets may not go where you want. A partner who was not married to, or in a civil partnership with, the deceased has no automatic right to inherit. You can find out how this would affect you at www.london-ifa.net/veronica-intestacy.

You should also create lasting powers of attorney. There are two types: financial and health. The first gives permission to your attorneys to act on your behalf regarding your financial matters if you are unable to do so – perhaps due to serious illness or dementia. The second allows your attorneys to instruct the doctors on your behalf if you are ill. Without one, should you become unable to act for yourself, no one can access your bank account to pay the bills or sign papers to sell a property. Your family will need to apply to the court of protection to appoint a deputy, which can take months to arrange and becomes expensive and onerous. In the meantime, you could be in limbo. So this should be put in place now.

6. Summary: your 10-point retirement plan

- Picture your retirement. Think about the pieces in your jigsaw.
- Work out your 'number' or numbers.
- Analyse where this could come from.
- Think about how much risk you are prepared to take to get there.
- Check out your pension and savings contracts.
- Work out the most tax-advantageous way to draw your income.
- Consider how this impacts on any inheritance tax or legacies.
- Make sure you have a safety net, if life throws you a curveball.
- Make sure you have lasting powers of attorney in place.
- Write your will – or check that it still says what you want.

Finally: enjoy your retirement!

VII. Another career?

Roderick Chamberlain
Career Guidance Services Limited

1. Introduction

The word 'retirement' has, in many quarters, developed a bad name. For every person who looks forward to the index-linked final salary pension and a succession of cruises, golf holidays and family indulgences, there is another who dreads the loss of earnings, lack of like-minded company, the buzz of the office and the corporate cut and thrust of professional or executive life. They see retirement as being condemned to quality time with the family, probably interspersed with gardening and conversations with neighbours with whom they have nothing in common.

Let's start, therefore, by asking what 'retirement' really means. At its simplest and truest level, retirement is the achievement of freedom of time and money.

Your time is now in your own control, not that of your clients, colleagues and other stakeholders in your life. You can do with it what you will. You don't have to justify your use of it to anyone except perhaps the close family – and to your own, typically misplaced, worker-bee conscience. We shall look later in the chapter at how hard it is to adjust to measuring days by quality rather than quantity.

Your money is your own to take, nurture and use. You are, in the words of a happy recent pensioner, being paid not to work. You are free to do what you will with however much or little money you have built up through your working life.

However, in thinking about both your time and your money, there will be existing commitments or ambitions you will need to take into account. There will be aspects, particularly in the financial world, where you are likely to need some serious professional advice. Every piece of that freedom described above can for some people be uncertain and confusing, if not downright scary.

So how might you start thinking about retirement in a way that works for rather than against you – a way that prepares you for it whether it comes at a time of your own or of somebody else's choosing? How do you make friends with it?

Retirement is truly no different from any other actual or prospective career move at any stage of your working life. From the ages of about 25 to about 65, we all ask ourselves at some juncture the same two questions:

- "How should I think about the rest of my career?" and
- "What should I do about it?"

There is a subsidiary question of relevance to retirement: "When should I do it?"

These questions are so glaringly obvious that we usually don't notice them until too late; indeed, many of us outsource our whole careers, and therefore to a large extent our lives, to an organisation which, in its mercy or otherwise, may deliver us greater or lesser fortune in what we achieve over anything up to 40 years. Bizarre, but true.

Things are different nowadays – particularly since the introduction of personal, portable pensions which have made mid-career people mobile. And today's working generations have a much looser, more even-handed approach to an employment contract as a meeting of equal partners. They too, however, face those questions, – even perhaps earlier and more often than previous generations, for which the options were more limited.

To answer these killer questions, one needs to develop three things, in order:

- first, a good understanding of yourself;
- next, a strategy to define the balance of activities you want to pursue; and
- finally, the tactics to see that strategy through.

Those wise and disciplined enough to have all these matters sorted out already to their full satisfaction need read no further. You are very blessed and will enjoy the fruits of your forethought. This chapter is intended for those who see the prospect of retirement less clearly and easily, to lay out for them a pathway to setting a strategy and some hints on the tactics for implementing it. We shall start with timing.

2. "When should I do it?"

Let's begin at the end, looking towards the date when you actually take retirement.

Once your leaving date is fixed, you risk remaining attached to the firm by three cords:

- Physical: Do you have to turn up in the office every day, even with an empty diary?
- Financial: Have you agreed terms? Are they acceptable? Do you have a trusted financial adviser?
- Emotional: Are you genuinely at peace with your departure?

Each of these cords is a consumer of mental space – a barrier to a fully focused concentration on the future. Each needs to be definitively cut before you can move on.

"So how might you start thinking about retirement in a way that works for rather than against you – a way that prepares you for it whether it comes at a time of your own or of somebody else's choosing? How do you make friends with it?"

So, to the extent that it is within your control, the obvious advice about timing is to start planning earlier than you might have thought in order to avoid leaving it too late: as the old military adage has it, "Time spent on reconnaissance is rarely wasted." The more homework you can do in advance, the better prepared you will be when the time comes and the more likely it is that your plans – dreams, even – will be fulfilled.

Law firms in particular have at least historically tended to retain partners several years longer than is truly beneficial for either party. While they have no doubt done this out of a misplaced sense of obligation ("Oh, but s/he's our partner!"), and while a partner is naturally tempted to hang on because of the financial advantages and sense of belonging and purpose, this can have the perverse effect of ensuring that people go at precisely the point when they are least employable.

So, start planning early – certainly in financial terms by age 45, so as to be prepared if you choose or are asked to go at or soon after 50. Good financial advice is worth the investment and careful planning will repay itself well: families can be complicated and expensive organisms, we are all living longer and not many things are getting cheaper.

"The more homework you can do in advance, the better prepared you will be when the time comes and the more likely it is that your plans – dreams, even – will be fulfilled."

But it is not our task in this chapter to look at money; we are concerned with time. And that 50-year age marker is interesting, because it seems to be a common point for more or less compulsory retirement. This sort of timescale enables people to contemplate at least one serious long-term career elsewhere. As one person put it: "I have a golden decade of usefulness.". If you stay until 60 or beyond, the same questions will apply, although the answers will probably be different.

3. "How should I think about it?"

3.1 Understanding yourself

A good understanding of yourself in this context is less about traditional strengths and weaknesses – important though they are for selling yourself when the time comes – than about your beliefs and values, behaviours and habits, expectations and instincts. The vital question is not "What am I good at?" but "What do I enjoy?"

This is the key to working out what sort of environment and what sort of occupation you will seek out, because the more you enjoy something, the more likely you are to succeed at it. After all, none of the Ten Commandments says, "Thou shalt be miserable."

In terms of work, it is remarkable that, time and again, people accept jobs on the basis of the brand, the pay, the responsibility, the product, the strategy; yet they do absolutely no due diligence on the most important question of all: what will it feel like to go to work each day? Is it fun to be in the office or around the boardroom table?

So, a random and far from exhaustive list of questions might include: do you prefer to work in open plan or an office? Doors open or shut? A formal or relaxed workplace atmosphere? On your own or with others? Lots of meetings or none? Do you welcome interest in your work from others and feel able and welcome to discuss theirs?

In terms of hobbies and spare time, some questions might be: do you relax energetically or sedentarily (eg, cycling or crosswords)? Indoors or out? Alone or in family or other company? If these activities include extensive travel, how much (for it will obviously affect your availability for work)?

All these matters will help you to piece together a quilt which becomes a satisfying, often varied, new life. It's time to start sewing the patchwork.

3.2 Formulating strategy

A tried and trusted way to address this – invented, as it happens, for the outgoing finance and operations director of a major City law firm, is the 'Wheel of Fortune' approach. Those of a certain age may recall the television game show.

This is a deceptively simple-looking tool for developing your strategy, forcing you to address all parts of your life and think about their relative importance to you. The segments of the wheel below show the ways in which you can choose to spend your time.

Let's have a look:

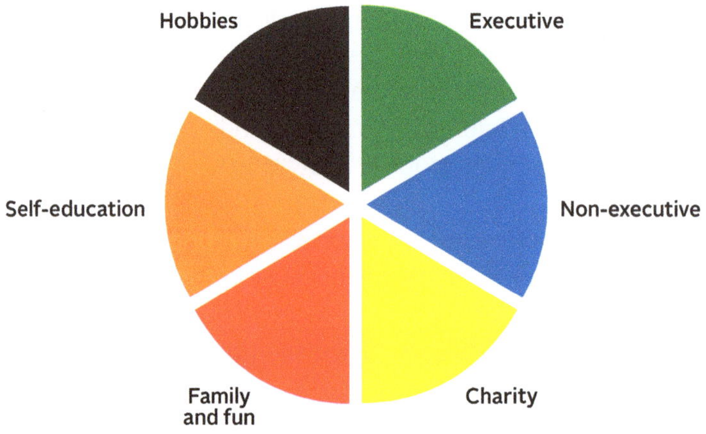

First let us consider these six segments, which encapsulate all the elements of life you will need to consider. The precise form of the wheel was developed through a series of monthly workshops on the topic over two or three years; some segments were fiercely debated before the version you see was settled. We begin at the top right-hand side:

- Executive: This segment embraces any and all paid work you may undertake in full or part-time employment, including self-employment or your own business.
- Non-executive: This includes all director's fees for paid non-executive work on private, public or not-for-profit boards.
- Charity: This includes any unpaid work as a volunteer or trustee (memorably defined as "a volunteer who goes to jail").
- Hobbies: Churchill had bricklaying and painting; Vince Cable had ballroom dancing; King George V had stamp collecting. You will have your own – or will need to find one.
- Self-education: This means learning, not teaching – CPD by another name.
- Family and fun: There was much robust discussion about whether these two belong together!

Now set against each segment the percentage of your time which you currently spend, or most recently spent, on each. Infuriatingly, those percentages must add up to exactly 100, so it is common for busily committed professionals and senior executives to find zeros or even negative figures – particularly in the 'family and fun' slice. It is a sad reflection of how our work, or at least our working day, can consume us – and an indicator of the opportunities ahead to blossom more widely.

Once you have done this, and reflected on the result, cast your mind forward to the point when your life in retirement will be running as well as you can imagine it. Repeat the exercise, remembering once again that the numbers have to total 100.

The differences show where you will need to focus your efforts to change the pattern of your days. It is no coincidence that the three right-hand segments represent 'work' and the left-hand segments 'leisure' or 'play', for you need to be sure to give full consideration to each. Don't let the 'family and fun' piece become the balancing item in the account.

Once you have done this, you have your strategy. Almost certainly, you will need to play quite extensively with the second part before you are satisfied with it. It will require consultation with – and indeed, the buy-in of – your family and any significant others in your life; it will have to be reality-checked against your financial situation and prospects; and, like all good plans, it is likely to end up looking rather different from what you anticipated. "The longest chapter in the book of life is called Stuff Happens." But you now have a goal which enables you to move on to the tactics of making it all happen.

There are no rules about how to set about this, beyond some simple and obvious ones:

- Be coruscatingly honest with yourself. If you fall into the trap of wondering or listening to what you think other people are sure you ought to want to do, you will forget to ask what you actually want to do. You fool only yourself if you deny yourself, and it will not end happily or well.
- Don't pre-disqualify ideas. Often people will say, "I won't go for this because I won't like it because..." or "I won't go for that because they won't want me because...". However, the most superficial examination shows that they do not yet have the evidence to reach such a conclusion. So be sure you have really run each opportunity to earth and done your due diligence before you reject the idea.
- In 2009 George Clooney starred in a movie called *Up in the*

> *Air* about outplacement and dealing with people made redundant from their firms. It was an appalling misrepresentation of the great work that such consultants do, but it did have one redeeming line of immense power: Clooney asks a retirement-age clerk, who has just been brutally fired, "Fred, what dreams have you left behind?"

This question can unlock many great ideas (in the movie, Fred sets up a business making barbeque equipment), which can fit into a number of the segments: people remember early ambitions to be lecturers, mentors, students of a given subject, athletes... And now is the time to do it. "If I am not for me, who will be for me?" And "if not now, when?"

4. "What should I do about it?"

It is beyond the brief of this chapter to delve into the detailed tactics of putting into effect your individual strategy for life in retirement, for it is axiomatic that this will be a highly personal process for each individual. Nevertheless, here are some observations and thoughts which have general application and which may serve as a guide as you approach this:

- From observation over the years, people tend to declare victory with four to six serious roles. More roles, unless they are very light touch, will be hard to fulfil with appropriate diligence; fewer may, at least in the early years, leave a frustrating amount of time free.

  Again from observation, achieving the right combination of four to six roles takes between 18 and 24 months from a standing start. Some people get there faster, but usually find that they accepted one without due care and attention. The joy of this life is that it is much easier to walk away from a non-executive job than it is from full-time, formal employment. (The exception is when the organisation is the subject of negative public scrutiny.)

- For lawyers who want to stay involved in the law, here are some options:
  - government department legal teams;
  - charity boards (see below for more about charities);
  - the wider world of not-for profit (local, national, supranational);
  - in-house counsel (a vast range of industries and sectors);
  - consulting (including headhunting); and
  - private practice at a different size/location/level (one client became the outsourced corporate and commercial department for half a dozen one or two-partner firms).

"The world of charities is often a good way into non-executive roles, so it is important to have a good set of triage processes to find your way through the thickets of opportunity."

- Many people start their own business – either a fully fledged law firm or a consultancy of some kind. This is a subject as broad and deep as retirement and a second or portfolio career. For starters, here are a few points to consider – questions with answers which will differ for different people:
  - Are you starting a business which you wish to survive and grow, as your legacy? Or is it a lifestyle choice for fun and some money in the autumn of your career?
  - If this 'executive' work sits at the core of your portfolio, how will that affect the time you have for other roles and activities – the other segments of the Wheel of Fortune above?
  - Have you understood the tax positions of sole traders, limited companies and limited and unlimited partnerships, so as to allow you to decide the most appropriate structure for you? Make sure you have an excellent tax accountant with whom you are on first-name terms.
  - Are you in all senses prepared for the marketing and sales effort you will need to give the business legs?

- The world of charities is often a good way into non-executive roles, so it is important to have a good set of triage processes to find your way through the thickets of opportunity. Charities can be local (eg, a hospice), national (eg, National Trust; Marie Curie)

About the authors

Ivor Adair
Partner, Fox & Partners
iadair@foxlawyers.com

Ivor Adair is a partner at Fox & Partners. He frequently acts in contentious partnership and high-value senior executive disputes. He regularly advises professional partners in the legal, accountancy and financial services sector. He has a particular interest in incentive arrangement disputes in the financial services sector and in business protection from employee/partner competition. He has considerable experience advising on sensitive and complex discrimination and whistleblowing claims.

Paul Beber
Consultant – professional practices, Cecil Associates
paulbeber@cecilassociates.co.uk

Paul Beber is a highly experienced chartered accountant. He qualified in 1978 with Arthur Young McClelland Moores (now EY) in Newcastle, then moved to its London office to develop wider experience. In 1980 he joined HW Fisher, a leading London-based, medium-sized practice, becoming a partner in 1982. After nearly 40 years with HW Fisher, he is retiring from the partnership in April 2020 and has established his own independent consultancy, Cecil Associates.

Paul's clients appreciate his strong commercial and financial acumen, and his invaluable help in problem solving, finding focused solutions and assisting with implementation. He specialises in advising entrepreneurial and family companies, as well as partnerships, on business development, structuring issues, succession management, acquisitions and disposals. He also advises and mentors individual professional partners on their development and issues they face. He is based in central London.

Roderick Chamberlain
Founding director, Career Guidance Services Limited
roderickchamberlain@gmail.com

A career guidance consultant since 2000, Rod Chamberlain has engaged with several hundred executives and professionals from a wide range of industries, sectors and countries as they worked their way through significant career change.

Rod was a banker in his earlier career. He has held executive committee and local board roles in investment, corporate and retail banks and securities firms owned by organisations of 11 different nationalities. His board experience spans three decades and five countries, with advisory and non-executive roles in the commercial, not-for-profit and voluntary sectors.

Mr Chamberlain holds an MBA from INSEAD and an MA in economics from Cambridge University. He has also acquired a certificate in occupational testing from the British Psychological Society and the Islamic Finance Qualification. He has lived, to work or study, in Germany, France, Australia and both coasts of the United States.He is fluent in German and French, with smatterings of other languages.

Caroline Field
Partner, Fox & Partners
cfield@foxlawyers.com

Caroline Field is a partner and head of Fox & Partners' litigation practice. She frequently acts on high-value and sensitive senior executive and partner moves. She advises professional partners and firms, typically in the legal, consultancy and financial services sectors, on a wide range of issues. Caroline frequently acts for professional firms in connection with the expulsion, compulsory retirement or de-equitisation of members or partners and for individuals responding to such processes. She regularly advises on the strategic handling of partner conduct, performance issues, discrimination and whistleblowing complaints. Caroline has a particular interest in advising on business protection from employee/partner competition.

She has successfully obtained and defended injunction applications and brought complex disputes to a successful conclusion following trial and alternative dispute resolution.

Ronnie Fox
Partner, Fox & Partners
rdfox@foxlawyers.com

Ronnie Fox helped to achieve recognition for employment law and partnership law as discrete areas of specialisation. Following the Industrial Relations Act 1971, he developed a reputation for advising on golden handshakes: his *Payments on Termination of Employment* was first published in 1981. The formation of the Employment Lawyers Association in 1992 encouraged growth in the number of employment lawyers, prompting him to focus on partnership law; in 1998 he founded and became the first chairman of the Association of Partnership Practitioners.

Ronnie founded and led two highly regarded law firms which bear his name. His contributions to the development of the law and the profession include working on many Law Society and International Bar Association (IBA) committees; chairing the IBA Senior Lawyers' Committee; receiving a Distinguished Service Award from and becoming Master of the City of London Solicitors' Company; and writing chapters of five law books and over 200 published articles.

Micheline Hogan
Psychodynamic psychotherapist
talk.one2one@gmail.com

Micheline Hogan is an experienced psychodynamic psychotherapist who trained at the Tavistock Clinic in London and worked for NHS Camden and Islington Trusts in both psychological and psychotherapy services. She has many years of experience in private clinical practice based in Golders Green, offering both brief and long-term psychotherapy. In addition to a clinical practice, she co-facilitated experiential medical groups focusing on the awareness of the emotional impact on the doctor-patient relationship. She designs resilience workshops, centred on the same principle but for client-lawyer relationships at law firms that specialise in family law or dispute resolution. Micheline is a French speaker and has citizenship in both the United Kingdom and France. She is a member of the Tavistock Society of Psychotherapists & Allied Professionals and the British Psychoanalytic Council.

Veronica Mann
Chartered financial planner, Talis Financial Advisers
vm@talisifa.com

Veronica Mann BSc, CFPTM Chartered MSCI is a chartered and certified financial planner. She specialises in independent financial advice which includes lifestyle planning, inheritance tax mitigation, retirement planning – with and without pensions – family protection and equity release.

Using her 30 years of experience in all aspects of wealth creation and protection, Veronica focuses on helping her clients protect their estates from tax and care fees. The goal is for them to achieve and maintain a comfortable, stress-free and financially secure position, particularly in their later years (she is an accredited member of the Society of Later Life Advisers).

Veronica's primary role is working with clients to understand what they want from life and creating a structured action plan to help them answer the question: "Will I run out of money?" She works mainly with people going through milestone life-changing events such as retirement, bereavement or divorce.

Nicky Owen
Partner, Crowe U.K. LLP
nicky.owen@crowe.co.uk

Nicky Owen is a tax partner specialising in professional practices at Crowe U.K.. She has worked with professional firms and partners her entire career, covering the spectrum of professional firms, from small husband and wife practices to magic circle law firms.

Nicky enjoys building rapport with her clients and helping them to understand their tax position throughout their journey as a partner, appreciating that their financial and tax position will evolve along the way. She advises partners on income tax, capital gains tax, inheritance tax, residence and non-domicile issues, principal private residence planning and pension planning.

Nicky runs roundtable discussions and seminars on tax and financial planning for retired partners and those planning their retirement.

Corinne Staves
Partner, Maurice Turnor Gardner LLP
corinne.staves@MTGLLP.com

Corinne Staves specialises in advising on partnerships, limited partnerships, LLPs and their uses for professional firms, financial services businesses and wealth planning vehicles. This includes partner and team moves, governance, regulation and the full range of transactions, such as launching new businesses, restructurings, mergers/demergers and LLP conversions. She advises both firms and individual partners.

Corinne is chair of the Association of Partnership Practitioners and regularly writes and speaks on partnership and LLP issues. She is ranked as a top-tier practitioner, with directories highlighting she is "a compassionate yet authoritative adviser ... always brilliantly prepared, but can think on her feet and delivers the results clients look for".

About Globe Law and Business

Globe Law and Business was established in 2005, and from the very beginning we set out to create law books which are sufficiently high level to be of real use to the experienced professional, yet still accessible and easy to navigate. Most of our authors are drawn from Magic Circle and other top commercial firms, both in the UK and internationally.

Our titles are carefully produced, with the utmost attention paid to editorial, design and production processes. We hope this results in high-quality books which are easy to read, and a pleasure to own. All our new books are also available as ebooks, which are compatible with most desktop, laptop and tablet devices.

We have recently expanded our portfolio to include a new range of journals and Special Reports, available both digitally and in hard copy format, and produced to the same high standards as our books.

We'd very much like to hear from you with your thoughts and ideas for improving what we offer. Please do feel free to email me at sian@globelawandbusiness.com with your views.

Sian O'Neill
Managing director
Globe Law and Business